LIFE IS SWEETER WITH JESUS

FROM THE MESSAGES OF ADRIAN ROGERS

Life is Sweeter with Jesus (Bible Study)

Published by Love Worth Finding Ministries, Inc.
              2941 Kate Bond Road
              Memphis, TN 38133-4017
              (800) 274-5683

Copyright © 2023 Love Worth Finding Ministries, Inc. All rights reserved. No part of this publication may be reproduced, stored in a retrieval system, or transmitted in any form by any means, electronic, mechanical, photocopy, recording or otherwise, without the prior permission of the publisher, except as provided by USA copyright law.

This Bible study is taken from Pastor Adrian Rogers' message series, *The Sweetest Fellowship This Side of Heaven*.

Scripture taken from the New King James Version.® Copyright © 1982 by Thomas Nelson. Used by permission. All rights reserved.

Printed in the United States of America

CONTENTS

INTRODUCTION 1

WEEK 1
Fellowship 3

WEEK 2
Sin 17

WEEK 3
New Birth 31

WEEK 4
Maturity 45

WEEK 5
The World 59

WEEK 6
The End 73

WEEK 7
Heaven 87

WEEK 8
Salvation 101

WEEK 9
Love 115

WEEK 10
Antichrists 129

WEEK 11
Assurance 143

LISTEN NOW 156

DISCUSSION GUIDE 157

INTRODUCTION

LIFE IS SWEETER WITH JESUS

If you long to experience the sweetness of life with Jesus, studying 1 John can help you know what you need to believe to experience abundant life. You will understand the beauty of fellowship with God and others and discover a depth of love that surpasses human understanding. The book of 1 John holds the keys to beginning a transformative journey in your Christian walk.

John was known as "the beloved disciple" and was one of the three disciples who were very close to Jesus. He wrote five books of the Bible: the gospel of John, the Book of Revelation, and 1-3 John. The three epistles of 1-3 John were written to confirm the saints so that they could know the truth. These letters contain themes of knowledge, fellowship, and life and give us the truths we need to anchor our faith so that we can know that what we have believed is true.

The simple, straightforward language of John's writing helps us clearly understand the spiritual truths that lead to a sweeter life with Jesus. We experience this in fellowship with God and others. We can understand how faith leads to a righteousness that saves us from our sins. We can learn how the Holy Spirit works in and through our lives. We can experience God's love more fully so that we can share His love with others. We can have the assurance that we are saved and belong to God. Through John's testimony, you are invited to taste the sweeter life that only Jesus brings.

WANT MORE?
The audio messages by Pastor Adrian Rogers from which this study is derived are linked using the QR code on page 156 at the end of this study.

WEEK 1

FELLOWSHIP

INTRODUCTION

The Apostle John wrote five books of the Bible. In the Gospel of John, the purpose was to convince sinners and to lead them to faith in Christ. In Revelation, the purpose was to comfort saints, help them understand the days in which they are living, and give believers hope for the Second Coming of the Lord Jesus. The epistles of 1, 2, and 3 John were written to confirm the saints. That's what we'll be studying.

> **That which was from the beginning, which we have heard, which we have seen with our eyes, which we have looked upon, and our hands have handled, concerning the Word of life—the life was manifested, and we have seen, and bear witness, and declare to you that eternal life which was with the Father and was manifested to us—that which we have seen and heard we declare to you, that you also may have fellowship with us; and truly our fellowship is with the Father and with His Son Jesus Christ. And these things we write to you that your joy may be full (1 John 1:1-4).**

True living is full and free in the Lord Jesus Christ. John witnessed this in person during his time with Jesus; he was one of His closest disciples. He wanted the saints to know how to experience this kind of life.

PRAY OVER IT

Dear God, I know that You offer abundant life with sweet fellowship, but I often find myself just going through the motions. My heart longs for more, and I know that longing comes from You. Open my eyes to see Your goodness and open my ears to hear Your Word. In Jesus' Name, Amen.

DAY 1

A FACT ESTABLISHED

▪ PONDER IT

John talked about a wonderfully sweet fellowship that comes through the life that we have with the Lord Jesus Christ. You can exist and not have life. The Bible talks about this as being spiritually dead, even while you are physically alive.

> **But she who lives in pleasure is dead while she lives (1 Timothy 5:6).**

The walking dead is not just science fiction; it's a reality that many people live out. Jesus said:

> **"The thief does not come except to steal, and to kill, and to destroy. I have come that they may have life, and that they may have it more abundantly" (John 10:10).**

Jesus was talking to people whose hearts were beating and who had blood flowing through their veins. But Jesus told them that they didn't have life. We are not just physical beings; we are also spiritual beings. To truly live, we need not only physical life, but spiritual life as well.

To enjoy a full and free life, the Apostle John tells us that **a fact must be established.**

> **That which was from the beginning, which we have heard, which we have seen with our eyes, which we have looked upon, and our hands have handled, concerning the Word of life (1 John 1:1).**

In John's day, there was a group of false teachers called the Gnostics. Their name comes from the Greek word "gnosis," which means "to know." These people felt they had superior knowledge. They did not believe God could have come to Earth in human flesh. They believed anything physical or material was evil. Therefore, they believed the true Messiah could not have had a material, physical body. They believed Jesus was a ghost or phantom that did not have a physical body.

John begins this letter by confronting Gnosticism. He shows the believers that Jesus Christ literally, physically, and bodily walked here on this Earth, and John was an eyewitness.

Just as there were false teachers in John's day, there are false teachers and cults in our day. The key identifier of a cult is what its followers believe about Jesus Christ. Mormons do not believe Jesus is the same person as God the Father. Jehovah's Witnesses do not believe Jesus is co-equal and co-eternal with Almighty God. John's inspired words help us deal with the cults of today.

> **Whoever transgresses and does not abide in the doctrine of Christ does not have God. He who abides in the doctrine of Christ has both the Father and the Son. If anyone comes to you and does not bring this doctrine, do not receive him into your house nor greet him (2 John 1:9-10).**

> **Jesus said to him, "I am the way, the truth, and the life. No one comes to the Father except through Me" (John 14:6).**

People who are wrong about Jesus don't know God. If we don't accept the fact of Jesus, then we can't have the life God offers.

PUT IT IN WRITING

- Are you spiritually alive or dead? How do you know?
- How have you heard other religions question or discount the deity and humanity of Jesus?

> Friend, if they're wrong about Jesus, it doesn't matter what they're right about.
>
> ADRIAN ROGERS

DAY 2

AN ETERNAL FACT AND A PHYSICAL FACT

PONDER IT

Jesus is an eternal fact. In both John's first epistle and the Book of John, he starts by establishing who Jesus is, a person of fact, existing since the beginning. Jesus is God's first Word.

> **That which was from the beginning (1 John 1:1a).**
>
> **In the beginning was the Word, and the Word was with God, and the Word was God (John 1:1).**

A word is the expression of an invisible thought or an idea. Jesus is the visible expression of the invisible God. Jesus articulates God. He is God's first word. He was there in the beginning. He is God's full word.

> **"I am the Alpha and the Omega, the Beginning and the End," says the Lord, "who is and who was and who is to come, the Almighty" (Revelation 1:8).**

The first and last letters of the Greek alphabet are alpha and omega. In the English alphabet, the first and last letters are A and Z. A library filled with English books may have thousands of books; all of them are made up of just 26 letters. Every thought in such a library came into existence through 26 letters. Jesus is saying that He is God's alphabet. Anything that God's going to say, He's going to say through Jesus. Jesus is God's first word, God's full word, and God's final word.

> **God, who at various times and in various ways spoke in time past to the fathers by the prophets, has in these last days spoken to us by His Son, whom He has appointed heir of all things, through whom also He made the worlds (Hebrews 1:1-2).**

Jesus is also a physical fact. He's not a phantom or a ghost. We have the testimony of evidence from John and others.

> **That which was from the beginning, which we have heard, which we have seen with our eyes, which we have looked upon, and our hands have handled, concerning the Word of life (1 John 1:1).**

John used the Greek word "theaomai," which means "to look carefully." John says he was with Jesus for three years. He watched Him and saw Him. There was audible, visible, and physical evidence. He had actual physical dimensions: height, weight, eye color, and hair color. Jesus Christ was in human form. He was born of a virgin, and He was a man, not just a spirit or phantom.

It's as much a heresy to deny the humanity of Jesus as it is to deny the deity of Jesus. He was God, not half God and half man. He wasn't all God and no man. He wasn't all man and no God. He was the God-man, all man and all God. Never has another like the Lord Jesus Christ existed.

Jesus is our Redeemer because He's human. He's our example because He's human. He's our comforter and friend because He's human. We don't have a high priest who cannot be touched with the feeling of our infirmities. He was tempted in all points like we are, yet without sin. He knows, He cares, and He understands.

> **For we do not have a High Priest who cannot sympathize with our weaknesses, but was in all points tempted as we are, yet without sin (Hebrews 4:15).**

PUT IT IN WRITING

- Why are these facts so important in the Christian faith? What would it mean if they were not true?
- In what ways was Jesus unlike us? In what ways was He like us?

> When you've said Jesus,
> you've said it all.
>
> ADRIAN ROGERS

DAY 3

A SPIRITUAL FACT

PONDER IT

Not only is Jesus an eternal fact and a physical fact, but **He is also a spiritual fact.**

> **...the life was manifested, and we have seen, and bear witness, and declare to you that eternal life which was with the Father and was manifested to us (1 John 1:2).**

The people John wrote to didn't see Jesus before His death, so John told them what he saw and heard. Even though you have never seen, heard, or touched Jesus, you can believe in Him. He is a spiritual fact that the Holy Spirit of God reveals. Our faith in John's testimony becomes the ears, eyes, and hands of our souls.

> **If we receive the witness of men, the witness of God is greater; for this is the witness of God which He has testified of His Son (1 John 5:9).**

An atheist professor ridiculed his Christian students by asking them if anyone had ever heard God. Nobody answered. He asked if anyone had ever seen God. Nobody answered. He asked if anyone had ever touched God. Nobody answered. He concluded, "There is no God." The class sat in silence.

But one student lifted his hand and said, "Professor, may I ask a question to the class?" After the professor gave permission, the student asked if anyone had ever heard the professor's brain. He asked if anyone had ever seen the professor's brain. He asked if anyone had ever touched the professor's brain. Nobody answered. He said, "Then, according to his own logic, we can conclude the professor has no brain."

PUT IT IN WRITING

- What testimony or witness of others helped convince you to believe the Gospel?
- How do you know Jesus was real? What argument would you give to someone who asks you to give a reason for your belief?

Remember the humanity of the Lord Jesus Christ; if you deny the humanity of Jesus, you're denying Christianity

ADRIAN ROGERS

DAY 4

A FELLOWSHIP EXPERIENCED

PONDER IT

Jesus' life is a fact established and **a fellowship experienced.** John saw it, and he shared it. Anybody who sees, hears, and knows it, wants to share it.

> **...that which we have seen and heard we declare to you, that you also may have fellowship with us; and truly our fellowship is with the Father and with His Son Jesus Christ (1 John 1:3).**

John witnesses so that we can have fellowship with God. The Greek word "koinonia" means "to hold things in common." Because of the established fact of Jesus, we can experience fellowship with God and with one another. We have fellowship with the Father and with His Son, Jesus Christ. John goes on to tell us what we have in common with the Father.

> **This is the message which we have heard from Him and declare to you, that God is light and in Him is no darkness at all. If we say that we have fellowship with Him, and walk in darkness, we lie and do not practice the truth (1 John 1:5-6).**

We're in the dark; He's in the light, and a great chasm separates us. So how can we have fellowship with God? God, who knew that there was a chasm between you and Himself, sent Jesus Christ to take on something that is common to us: human flesh. Jesus became a man, and He never discarded His deity. Because He became human, we began to have something in common. He took on the nature of Man so that we might take on the nature of God.

> **...by which have been given to us exceedingly great and precious promises, that through these you may be *partakers of the divine nature*, having escaped the corruption that is in the world through lust (2 Peter 1:4, emphasis added).**

The word "partaker" is the same word that is translated "fellowship" in 1 John. He took on our human nature so that we could partake of His divine nature. Because we have fellowship with God, we must have fellowship with one another. When you and a fellow believer are both born of God, the same nature that's in you is also in the other person. The Jesus in you loves the Jesus in that believer. We're born from the same womb, the womb of grace. The Bible calls it the "koinonia" of the Gospel or the fellowship of the Spirit.

I thank my God upon every remembrance of you, always in every prayer of mine making request for you all with joy, *for your fellowship in the gospel* from the first day until now (Philippians 1:3-5, emphasis added).

Therefore if there is any consolation in Christ, if any comfort of love, if any *fellowship of the Spirit*, if any affection and mercy, fulfill my joy by being like-minded, having the same love, being of one accord, of one mind (Philippians 2:1-2, emphasis added).

Our fellowship is with the Father and with one another. When you have the nature of God in you, you are born of the Spirit. As a partaker of the divine nature, you have this fellowship with God. Therefore, we should seek out business partners, spouses, and close friends who also have fellowship with God.

PUT IT IN WRITING
- When have you experienced fellowship with God and with others?
- What have you seen and heard that can only be explained through God?

> The Holy Spirit is to a Christian
> what instinct is to an animal.
>
> ADRIAN ROGERS

DAY 5

A FULLNESS ENJOYED

▫ PONDER IT

Jesus' life is a fact established and a fellowship experienced. Through Him, we can have **a fullness enjoyed.** There is no joy like the joy of knowing one another in Christ. John said he wrote this book so that we might have joy.

> **And these things we write to you that your joy may be full (1 John 1:4).**

A woman lost her house keys. She looked all over the house but couldn't find them. Finally, she looked in her purse where they should have been and found them. She was looking in the wrong places because her keys belonged in her purse. You can look all over for joy, but you won't find it until you find it in Jesus Christ. Joy is the byproduct of fellowship with God and fellowship with the family of God.

> **You will show me the path of life; in Your presence is fullness of joy; at Your right hand are pleasures forevermore (Psalm 16:11).**

We're not talking about happiness; we're talking about joy. Happiness depends upon what happens; joy depends upon the Lord. If you live for happiness, you're a prisoner of circumstances. If the circumstances change, then you're not happy anymore. But Jesus never changes, so His joy never ends. Happiness is cosmetic; it's on the outside. Joy is character; it is on the inside. Happiness only meets your surface needs, but joy meets your deepest needs. Happiness evaporates in a crisis. Joy often intensifies in a crisis. Happiness is wonderful. But happiness is at its fullest when it is mingled with the joy of the Lord.

PUT IT IN WRITING

- Where have you been looking for joy? What would it look like for you to find joy in the Lord?
- Which do you want more: happiness or joy? Why?

The reason we're called witnesses and not lawyers is because a lawyer argues a case, and a witness tells what he's seen and heard. The only person who can't witness is the person who hasn't seen or heard anything.

ADRIAN ROGERS

DAY 6

A FULLNESS ENJOYED

PRACTICE IT

Sin promises joy, but it never delivers. We have more entertainment, more amusements, more restaurants, but also more loneliness, more depression, more alcoholism, more drugs, more divorce, and more suicide than ever. We are looking in the wrong places because true joy is only found in the Lord Jesus Christ.

John said this joy-filled life comes from God, and it is real. It is a fact established, and it results in a fellowship experienced. Then there's a fullness in joy. We have joy unspeakable and full of glory. Jesus is the Word of God, speaking even today. He's telling you that He loves you.

Jesus is broadcasting His love for you. He is sending you messages of love. You wouldn't say that there's no Internet just because your Wi-Fi is turned off. Do you have your Wi-Fi on? Are you searching for a connection? Are you looking for a relationship with Jesus? He is here. He is the Word of life.

If you don't have this joy, the first step is to receive Jesus Christ as your Lord and Savior. You can pray a prayer like this:

> *Dear God, I know that You love me, and I know that You want to save me. Jesus, You died to save me. You promised to save me if I would trust You. I do trust You. Come into my heart, forgive my sin, cleanse me, save me.*
>
> *I thank You for saving me. I yield my life to You. I turn from all sin. I will follow You wherever You lead me if You will only help me. I'm weak, but You're strong. Begin now to make me the person You want me to be and help me never to be ashamed of You. Give me the courage to make my decision to follow You public. Thank you, Jesus, Amen.*

PROCLAIM IT

If you prayed to receive Christ, please share your decision with another Christian you know or with your pastor. We would also like to hear about it so that we can provide you with free resources to help you grow in your new faith. Please let us know by going to **lwf.org/discover-jesus,** scrolling down the page and clicking on I BELIEVE.

If you have received Christ, you have access to a joy-filled life. Just like John testified to what he saw and heard, it's time for you to share with others what you have seen and heard. Ask God to give you an opportunity this week to share with someone else what He has done in your life.

> Happiness is like a thermometer; it just registers conditions. Joy is the thermostat that controls the conditions.
>
> ADRIAN ROGERS

> When you do what John tells you, the only way that it can get sweeter is for us just to go to glory.
>
> ADRIAN ROGERS

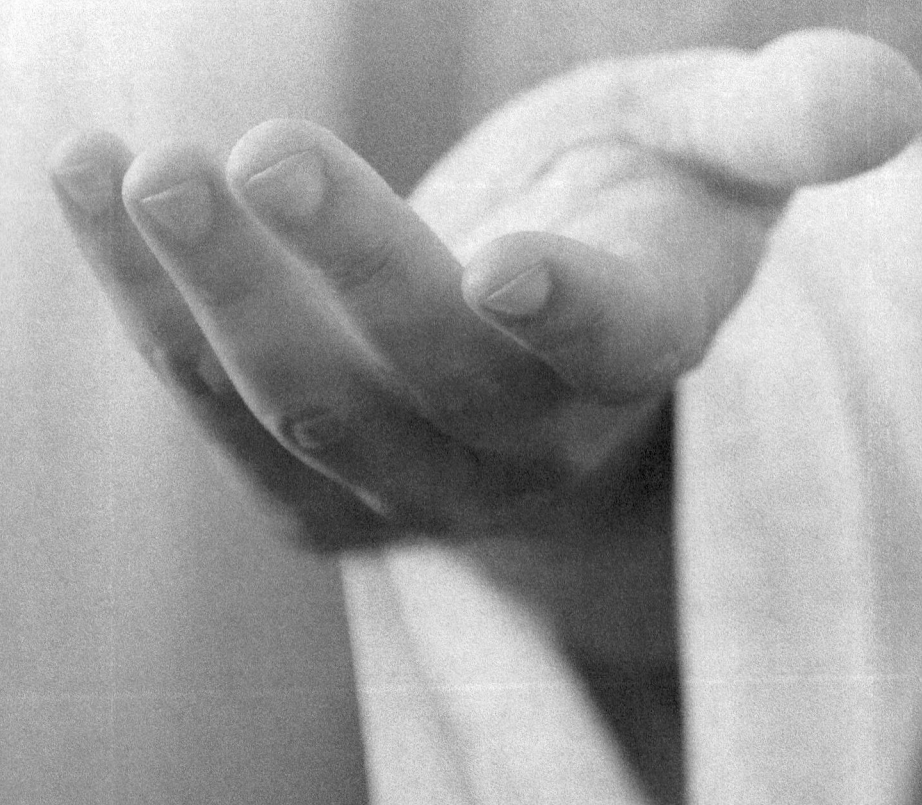

WEEK 2

SIN

INTRODUCTION

A little boy went into a drugstore and asked if he could borrow the telephone. The pharmacist gave him permission, and the boy dialed the grocery store. When the grocer answered, the boy asked if they needed a stock clerk—somebody who could stock the shelves, carry the packages, and sweep the floor. The man said they already had a boy who did that. The boy asked, "Well, does he do a good job? Maybe he's not adequate." The grocer said that their current store clerk was very adequate and that they were very satisfied. After the boy hung up, the pharmacist noticed that the boy didn't get the job. "No," the boy said, "I already have the job over there. I was just checking up on myself."

Every now and then you need to check up on yourself to see if there is anything in your heart keeping you from having fellowship with God. It is likely a sin or secret fault. The things we hide and disguise are things that keep us from God.

> **This is the message which we have heard from Him and declare to you, that God is light and in Him is no darkness at all. If we say that we have fellowship with Him, and walk in darkness, we lie and do not practice the truth (1 John 1:5-6).**

PRAY OVER IT

Dear God, I want to have fellowship with You, but sometimes I feel distant from You. Open my eyes this week to see the things in my heart and life that keep me from fellowship with You. Thank you for sending Your Son Jesus so that I could enjoy this fellowship with You. In Jesus' Name, Amen.

DAY 1

THE SIN PROBLEM

PONDER IT

Secret faults and hidden sins keep us from enjoying fellowship with God. This is why John encouraged the saints to live in the light and not in the darkness.

> ...God is light and in Him is no darkness at all. If we say that we have fellowship with Him, and walk in darkness, we lie and do not practice the truth. But if we walk in the light as He is in the light, we have fellowship with one another, and the blood of Jesus Christ His Son cleanses us from all sin (1 John 1:5-7).

The Bible is the only book in the world that addresses the problem of sin. The way to deal with sin is to first recognize sin for what it is. Our culture today doesn't even like the word sin; it's outdated and politically incorrect. It's more politically correct to call it a mistake or a misjudgment. But Jesus did not die for mistakes or misjudgments. Jesus died as an atonement for sin!

Behaviorists and psychologists want to reduce our behavior to the sum total of our genetics and our environment. In this thinking, man is not wicked; he's weak and needs to be strengthened. He's not sinful; he's sick and needs to be cured. He's not evil; he is ill and needs to be accommodated. People never deal with the problem of sin because they never get to the root of the problem. Spurred on by the theory of evolution, we've been taught that Man evolved and that all our actions are the results of genetics and environment.

However, mankind was created in the image of God, rejected God, and sinned willfully. Sin is not an accident or an incident; it is high treason against God. If you don't understand sin for what it is, you will never ever deal with sin. If you don't understand the severity of sin, you won't understand how much you need the remedy that God has provided.

The evolutionist believes we simply need more time, and we will evolve and progress out of sin. Education believes that if we teach people the right things in the right way, we can solve the sin problem. But colleges and universities today are rampant with sin and also with depression, anxiety, and suicide. Humanists believe people are naturally good and through self-actualization, we can eliminate sin. Sociology believes a change in environment would fix it, but even the best neighborhoods deal with crime. Humanity fell in the Garden of Eden, and there was no better environment. Psychology says that sin is nothing more than feelings of guilt that need to be resolved.

If you think that sin is merely a problem to be fixed, you will look for a solution other than forgiveness and cleansing. If it's an inconvenience, you will try to compensate for sin or commiserate with it. But if you want to have fellowship with God, you must deal with sin and call it what it is.

PUT IT IN WRITING

- What are some ways that our culture or other religions deal with the problem of sin?
- What do you think about sin? How have you experienced the impact of sin on your relationship with God?

> It seems that the only sin today is to call sin 'sin'.
>
> ADRIAN ROGERS

DAY 2

SIN & RELATIONSHIP

PONDER IT

God deals with our sin from the moment of repentance. When you receive Jesus Christ as your personal Lord and Savior by faith, when you repent of sin and trust Him, you are born again. As a result, that sin is dealt with legally forever.

> **"For I will be merciful to their unrighteousness, and their sins and their lawless deeds I will remember no more" (Hebrews 8:12).**

When you get saved, every sin—past, present, and future—is buried in the grave of God's forgetfulness.

> **"I, even I, am He who blots out your transgressions for My own sake; and I will not remember your sins" (Isaiah 43:25).**

When God says He will not remember our sins, it doesn't mean God cannot recall them. He is not talking about intellectual remembrance. When He remembers our sins, they are sins that have been forgiven and therefore no longer count against us. In the same way, we can never forget the sins we have committed, but when we remember our sins, we don't remember them as sins held against us. We remember them as sins forgiven and forgotten by the grace of God. If we're going to be saved, we've got to be saved by the grace of God.

> **"Blessed are those whose lawless deeds are forgiven, and whose sins are covered; blessed is the man to whom the Lord shall not impute sin" (Romans 4:7-8).**

God deals with our sins judicially and daily. We are saved by grace and kept by grace, and our sin is buried in the grave of God's forgetfulness. Yet when we sin each day, God looks at us with the eyes of a loving Father, not with the eyes of a judge.

We have two vital relationships as a Christian. One is sonship: we're born into the family of God. Our new lineage is established and will never change. Our birth into this spiritual family can never be undone. Once you're born into the family of God, you're in the family of God.

The other relationship is one that can change: it is fellowship. With our own parents, we have times and seasons when we are out of fellowship with them, even though we still have a relationship.

Ancestry is established by birth; fellowship is established by conduct. John is talking about the forgiveness of sin and the cleansing of our daily sins.

> **...that which we have seen and heard we declare to you, that you also may have fellowship with us; and truly our fellowship is with the Father and with His Son Jesus Christ (1 John 1:3).**

He's not talking about judicial or legal forgiveness here. He's talking about parental forgiveness. This is what Jesus Christ taught us when He taught us to pray by saying "Our Father in heaven...." (See Matthew 6:9.)

Many of you are saved and on the way to Heaven, but you're not enjoying that fellowship—the "koinonia." We can restore fellowship by getting rid of hidden sins that keep us from the Father's face; this brings sweet, wonderful fellowship with God.

PUT IT IN WRITING

- What sins are you having trouble believing are forgiven? How does it feel to know that your sins are forgotten?
- Sin does not affect your adoption as a son or daughter of God. How does sin impact your fellowship with God?

> If God were to put one half of one sin on my judicial record, one half of one sin would be enough to damn me and doom me forever.
>
> ADRIAN ROGERS

DAY 3

THE EVOLUTION OF A LIE

PONDER IT

We talked about the definition of sin and the impact of sin, but notice how God convicts of sin.

> **If we say that we have fellowship with Him, and walk in darkness, we lie and do not practice the truth. But if we walk in the light as He is in the light, we have fellowship with one another, and the blood of Jesus Christ His Son cleanses us from all sin.**
>
> **If we say that we have no sin,** *we deceive ourselves,* **and the truth is not in us. If we confess our sins, He is faithful and just to forgive us our sins and to cleanse us from all unrighteousness. If we say that we have not sinned,** *we make Him a liar,* **and His word is not in us (1 John 1:6-10, emphasis added).**

John is pointing out that we are saying one thing and doing another. We are pretending, and John is showing us the evolution of a lie.

You lie to deny sin. You know in your heart that you are playing a game. You're playing the church game. You're playing the role of a good Christian. You go to church, you teach a Bible class, or you sing in the choir. But there's a secret that you keep hidden so that no one else will see it. You don't treat it like it is a sin, and you keep quietly, secretly doing it.

You believe your own lie. You deceive yourself to the point that you believe you are without sin. But when you set out to deceive somebody else, you deceive yourself most of all. When you cannot even believe yourself, you blur the distinction between light and dark, between the truth and the lie. You've stonewalled God, moved in and out of fellowship with Him, and nothing seems to happen. You still sing in the choir; you still teach the class. You still go to church and shake hands with all the people. You start to believe that maybe it's not a sin at all. Maybe you are all right. Maybe it was just an error. Maybe it's a personality flaw. So, you begin to smooth over your sin.

You lie to God. When you call God a liar, you are the one who's lying because God cannot lie. If God brings you under conviction, instead of admitting it, you say it was a mistake, an error, or a negative environment. You convince yourself that it is legitimate resentment or righteous indignation. You don't let the Holy Spirit of God convict you of that sin. You have the audacity to lie to Almighty God and then call Him a liar.

We lie to deny sin, to deceive ourselves, and to defy the Savior. When we do that, fellowship is completely broken. We have stepped out of the light and into the darkness.

How does God bring you back? God will not bring you back unless you expose yourself to the light. If you stay in the darkness, you will never feel any conviction. But if you, as a beloved child of God, turn toward the light, God will shine the light of His holiness upon your life and bring you under conviction.

PUT IT IN WRITING

- How have you seen the evolution of a lie play out in your own life? What have you kept hidden from God?
- What does it look like in your life to walk in the light and not in the darkness?

> Jesus Christ is the Light. There is no reason for you to stumble in darkness when you can walk in the Light.
>
> ADRIAN ROGERS

DAY 4

THE CONVICTION OF SIN

PONDER IT

As a child of God, it is very, very, very important that you learn the difference between Holy Spirit conviction and Satanic accusation. The devil is the accuser of the brethren. The Holy Spirit is the one who loves us and convicts us. Because the devil is very clever, many people do not know the difference between conviction and accusation. Before you sin, the devil says, "Go ahead and do it, you can get away with it." After you sin, the devil tells you, "You'll never get away with it. He can't possibly take you back or love you." He will entice you to sin and then condemn you because you sinned. That is what accusation sounds like. That's not the Holy Spirit of God.

God is light, and there's nothing purer than light. When the Holy Spirit shines light upon you, you will come under conviction as a child of God. If you turn your face to the light, He will pull back the veil of darkness caused by those lies you've been telling yourself, and He will expose that sin. This is how the Holy Spirit of God convicts you.

God will convict you legitimately. He will never convict you over any sin that has been confessed and cleansed. If an old sin that you have confessed comes up again, it is not the Holy Spirit of God. The accuser goes back into your past and brings up sin that has been cleansed and forgotten. If it comes up again, it is the devil trying to bring you into double jeopardy. The Holy Spirit will never pull something from your past that's already been dealt with.

The Holy Spirit of God will convict you specifically. If the devil can't go into your past and drag up something, he will try to convict you vaguely. He will just make you feel bad, unworthy, or just no good. But you're not a poor, old, unworthy sinner; you're the righteousness of God in Christ. You're a child of God, a prince or princess. Jesus is not ashamed to call you His brothers and sisters! The devil wants to just make you feel that you're no good or unworthy. If you feel bad all over, that's just accusation from the accuser.

If you do something that has not been cleansed, forgotten, and buried in the grave of God's forgetfulness, the Holy Spirit will gently point it out. He will remind you that you just told a lie or were rude to someone. Like a good doctor, He will put His finger on the sore spot and gently push. If it hurts, it's a sign that it's not right.

The Holy Spirit of God will convict you redemptively. Accusation discourages you and drives you away from God. Accusation convinces you there's no path to redemption and you should quit trying. Conviction shows you what you have and reminds you that if you come to Jesus, He'll forgive you and cleanse you. The Holy Spirit encourages you to come back into fellowship because you're loved.

PUT IT IN WRITING

- Is the sin that you are feeling convicted of legitimate and specific? What is your response if the sin is from your past or vague?
- What is God reminding you about your sin today? Is it driving you away from God or drawing you back into fellowship with Him?

> Confess it once; praise Him
> a thousand times.
>
> ADRIAN ROGERS

DAY 5

THE CLEANSING OF SIN

PONDER IT

We talked about the conviction of sin, now let's shift to the cleansing of sin. Once the Holy Spirit of God convicts you of a particular sin in your heart and in your life legitimately, specifically, and redemptively, He draws you to Jesus.

If we confess our sins, He is faithful and just to forgive us our sins and to cleanse us from all unrighteousness (1 John 1:9).

This is not the judicial cleansing that we received when we were saved. This is talking about fellowship with God and about how God deals with our daily sin as His children.

In Greek, the word "confess" is "homologéō" which means "to say the same." A confession of sin is an agreement with God. It is saying with God what God says about that sin. It is not just saying, "Well, I did it, okay." That's not a confession; it's an admission. A confession of sin agrees with God that you have sinned. The Holy Spirit legitimately, specifically, redemptively convicts you of sin and puts His finger on it.

Because we broke down the process of conviction, let's break down the process of confession. How should you confess your sin?

Confess sin immediately. In the Greek language, the verb is in the present tense. It's not talking about something that you have done in the past; it is something that you keep doing. One translation says, "If we are continually confessing our sins." Confession ought to be a habit of our lives. You don't just confess your sins at the end of the day, the end of the week, or during the annual revival meeting. If you get a speck of dust in your eye, you try to get it out as soon as possible; you don't wait. Be sensitive to the conviction of sin and respond immediately.

Confess sin specifically. John says that we should confess our sins—plural. This is not about confessing that you have a sin nature. It's talking about what you did specifically. Call it by name. If you want to do business with God, you say, "God, forgive me for reading that dirty book. I dishonored You, my wife, and my own body. God, I put filth in my mind, I'm so sorry. I shouldn't have done it. God, I won't do it again. Forgive me." He will.

Confess sin confidently. God is faithful and just to forgive us. If He doesn't forgive you, He would be a liar and a crook. He would be unfaithful and unjust. If you agree with God, He will cleanse you from all unrighteousness. Sometimes the devil will tell you that you have done something so bad that it can't be forgiven. That's a lie out of Hell. There's no sin that the blood of Jesus Christ cannot cleanse.

...and the blood of Jesus Christ His Son cleanses us from all sin (1 John 1:7b).

Thank God for the double detergent of the precious blood of the Lord Jesus Christ! Not only does He forgive us of sin, but He also cleanses us from sin. He washes out the stain. It is gone, forgotten, and washed whiter than snow.

PUT IT IN WRITING

- What keeps you from immediately confessing your sin? What specific sins can you confess to God today?
- Are you confident that your sin has been forgiven? What keeps you from believing that God has forgiven you?

> You name it and nail it. "Forgive me, Lord, for that lie. Forgive me, Lord, for that selfishness. Forgive me, Lord, for that pride."
>
> ADRIAN ROGERS

DAY 6

THE CONQUEST OF SIN

PRACTICE IT

Lastly, we must consider the conquest of sin. Is God encouraging us to sin by writing this down? No, He is encouraging us not to sin.

> **My little children, these things I write to you, so that you may not sin. And if anyone sins, we have an Advocate with the Father, Jesus Christ the righteous. And He Himself is the propitiation for our sins, and not for ours only but also for the whole world (1 John 2:1-2).**

The word "advocate" is a fancy word for "lawyer." "Propitiation" is a fancy word for "satisfaction or atonement." Jesus satisfied the demands of a righteous and holy God. Christ died for everybody in the whole world, and He is faithful and just to forgive us our sins. He died for those sins that you are confessing.

God doesn't want us to be light and cavalier about our sins. When we live with Him, the love of God is perfected in us. (See 1 John 2:5.) A slave serves because he is required to. An employee serves because he needs to get money. A child of God serves because he wants to… because of the love of God. The fact that God saves us and then cleanses us should not encourage us to sin. The desire of our hearts is to never sin again. But if we sin, we have an Advocate and a Savior.

If people understood what we have in Jesus, you couldn't keep them away. So many people have stonewalled themselves against God. But God wants us to have fellowship with Him and fellowship with each other. (See 1 John 1:4, 7.)

Legal salvation is where God forgives your sins, never to bring them up against you anymore. You can have that today. You can become a child of God. You can become twice-born in a world of once-born people by receiving Jesus. If you want to do that, you can pray a prayer like this:

Dear God, I am a sinner. I cannot save myself. I need to be saved. My sin deserves judgment, but I want mercy. Jesus, You died to save me, You promised to save me if I would trust You. I do trust You with all of my heart. Come into my life, forgive my sin, cleanse me, save me, Jesus. In Jesus' Name, Amen.

PROCLAIM IT

If you prayed to receive Christ, please share your decision with another Christian you know or with your pastor. We would also like to hear about it so that we can provide you with free resources to help you grow in your new faith. Please let us know by going to **lwf.org/discover-jesus**, scrolling down the page and clicking on I BELIEVE.

Set aside some time in a quiet place to ask God to show you your sin. When the Holy Spirit convicts you of sin, confess it. Receive the forgiveness that is offered to you and walk in fullness of life. Ask God if you need to confess your sin to someone else and restore a relationship; then walk in obedience by faith.

Confession is faith turned inside out.

ADRIAN ROGERS

WEEK 3

NEW BIRTH

INTRODUCTION

A psychiatrist's nurse told him a man who thought he was invisible was in the waiting room. The doctor said, "Tell him we can't see him." Sometimes people think things about themselves that are not true. In the same way, some people make up things about Christianity. They say one thing but live another way.

When people are saved, they are born again, and they develop birthmarks or traits. When people are truly saved, they have characteristics that distinguish them from others who are not truly saved. But sometimes, people say one thing and live another. Their walk doesn't match their talk, and they don't have the birthmarks of a believer. Knowing the birthmarks will help you recognize whether you have been born again so that you can determine to know Jesus Christ.

Some think that Christianity is a matter of behavior modification, trying to be better and do better. Other people have the idea that Christianity is all negative, full of things not to do or say. The devil wants you to think negatively about God, to think that God is a cosmic killjoy, and that Christians are so strait-laced they can't have any fun in this life. Other people think that all Christians care about is going to Heaven and sitting around on fluffy clouds wearing wooly robes and plucking harps. There are caricatures or distorted pictures of Christianity. When you have Jesus Christ in your life, He gives you a life that is wonderful, abundant, and free.

PRAY OVER IT

Dear God, I don't want to be a person who says one thing and lives another way. This week, open my eyes to see the birthmarks of a true believer and examine my heart so I can see the truth about me. In Jesus' Name, Amen.

DAY 1

SUBMIT TO THE LORDSHIP OF JESUS

PONDER IT

Scripture tells us what a true believer looks like. In 1 John 2, the traits of a true believer are identified by the phrase "If we say." John tells us what a person who is saved would do. **A true believer is somebody who is submitted to the lordship of Jesus.**

Jesus is Lord, and He has a right to command us. If you say that you know Him and don't keep His commandments, you are a liar. You have never been saved.

> **Now by this we know that we know Him, if we keep His commandments. He who says, "I know Him," and does not keep His commandments, is a liar, and the truth is not in him (1 John 2:3-4).**

The word "keep" means "to value as you would value a treasure." If a friend were to give you something and ask you to keep it for him, you would guard it and protect it. Because it's valuable to your friend, you would respect it. In the same way, we are to respect and follow the commandments of God. They should be meaningful to us, not just blasé things we read or hear but don't retain or prioritize.

"Keep" was also a sailor's word. They didn't have global positioning satellites when this was written. Men who sailed across the trackless sea had to guide themselves by the stars. Those stars never changed, so a sailor could guide his ship across the ocean by "keeping the stars." He set his course by the stars, the things that never changed.

Those who are born again submit to the Lordship of Jesus and keep His commandments. They want to live their lives according to Jesus. They value, and steer their lives by, His commands.

This doesn't mean that you could never sin. A navigator steering the ship may get blown off course, may take his eyes from the stars and let the wheel turn in the wrong way. But when he sees what he's doing, he corrects the course. The desire of his heart is to steer by those stars.

Let the desire of your heart be to live by God's Word. The burning ambition of your life should be to please Him, to keep His Word, to keep His commandments. If it's not and you call yourself saved, the Bible calls you a liar.

To clarify, you are not saved by keeping the commandments. Breaking one doesn't mean you're not saved. You don't keep Jesus' commands because you are trying to work your way into Heaven. You do this because you love Jesus Christ and have submitted your life to Him.

But whoever keeps His word, truly the love of God is perfected in him. By this we know that we are in Him (1 John 2:5).

If you love Jesus Christ, you're going to obey Him and serve Him—not to earn your salvation, but because you love Him. There are times you've failed. There are times you've stumbled. But ultimately you desire to guard those commandments and steer your life by God's stars.

PUT IT IN WRITING

- Do you give deference to the commandments of God? What does it look like for you to guard and treasure the commandments of the Lord Jesus Christ?
- What is the difference between thinking you are saved based on what you do and understanding you're saved based on what Jesus did for you?

> These are not legal commandments;
> they're love commandments.
>
> ADRIAN ROGERS

DAY 2

SEEK THE LIFESTYLE OF JESUS

PONDER IT

True believers seek the lifestyle of Jesus. They walk as Jesus walked.

> **He who says he abides in Him ought himself also to walk just as He walked (1 John 2:6).**

The life of a believer ought to imitate the life of Christ. But we don't walk as Jesus walked to be saved. We walk as Jesus walked because as we abide in Him, His life is reproduced in us. We are to be as He is.

> **Love has been perfected among us in this: that we may have boldness in the day of judgment;** *because as He is,* **so are we in this world (1 John 4:17, emphasis added).**

This transformation doesn't happen when we get to Heaven, but it happens in this world as we follow Jesus' pattern for life. When we abide in Him, we walk as He walked. To do this, we must know how Jesus walked.

Jesus walks in the light. To walk in the light means that nothing is hidden. To walk in the light is to walk with honesty. Jesus was honest with the Father, with Himself, and with others. If you're living a lie, you're not walking as Jesus walked. If your heart is full of deceit and lies, you need to get saved. Not only did Jesus walk in honesty, but Jesus also walked in purity.

> **But if we walk in the light as He is in the light, we have fellowship with one another, and the blood of Jesus Christ His Son cleanses us from all sin (1 John 1:7).**

Jesus is pure. If He is pure, we are to be pure. If there's any impurity in your life, you are not following the lifestyle of Jesus. We cannot claim to be saved and fill our minds and hearts with inappropriate media and entertainment. Anything you wouldn't do or watch with Jesus sitting next to you shouldn't be done at all.

And everyone who has this hope in Him purifies himself, just as He is pure (1 John 3:3).

Jesus is righteous. When we abide in Him, He becomes our righteousness. Righteousness is not merely not doing certain things like stealing, getting drunk, or saying bad words. Jesus went about doing good. That was righteous. Everywhere He went He was doing good. That is the lifestyle of Jesus.

The people who were watching Jesus couldn't understand His life. But it was an open secret. Jesus simply did what the Father asked Him to do.

"For I have not spoken on My own authority; but the Father who sent Me gave Me a command, what I should say and what I should speak" (John 12:49).

Jesus was totally committed to the Father. When you follow Jesus the way Jesus followed the Father, Jesus will be to you what the Father was to Jesus. You're not just trying to imitate Jesus; you are abiding in Jesus.

PUT IT IN WRITING

- Are you walking in the light? Are you living a life that is honest, pure, and righteous? When you put your life in the light, what is revealed?
- What does it look like for you to abide in Jesus? What is the result?

> Obedience is a duty to be
> performed, a debt to be paid,
> a delight to be preferred, and
> a decision to be practiced.
>
> ADRIAN ROGERS

DAY 3

ABIDE IN JESUS

PONDER IT

The Bible says we are to walk as He walked, because as He is, so are we.

> ...as He is, so are we in this world (1 John 4:17b).

> **He who says he abides in Him ought himself also to walk just as He walked (1 John 2:6).**

The secret of walking as Jesus walked is to abide in Jesus. You are to abide in Christ just like a branch abides in a vine. This is how Jesus explained it in the Gospel of John:

> **"Abide in Me, and I in you. As the branch cannot bear fruit of itself, unless it abides in the vine, neither can you, unless you abide in Me. I am the vine, you are the branches. He who abides in Me, and I in him, bears much fruit; for without Me you can do nothing" (John 15:4-5).**

This is a life of full relinquishment. The branch is totally connected to the vine. It is surrendered to and dependent on the vine. That's what it means to abide in Him. A branch has no side issues that the vine doesn't know about.

Some of you have side issues that you try to keep separate from your relationship with God. You think your job obligations or your desire for a nice vacation don't have to be submitted to Jesus. All you can do is serve Jesus. If you use your job right, you'll be serving Jesus with your job. You can serve Jesus with your family and with your recreation. When you abide in Christ, you don't have any side issues. The Apostle Paul said he had one goal and one prize:

> **...but one thing I do, forgetting those things which are behind and reaching forward to those things which are ahead, I press**

toward the goal for the prize of the upward call of God in Christ Jesus (Philippians 3:13b-14).

Jesus said:

"No one can serve two masters; for either he will hate the one and love the other, or else he will be loyal to the one and despise the other. You cannot serve God and mammon" (Matthew 6:24).

This is a life of reliance. The branch doesn't depend upon anything else except the vine. Everything the branch needs, the vine supplies. When it's harvest time, the branch doesn't worry about how many grapes there are, what size, what color, or how sweet they are. All the branch does is bear the grapes. It has one thing to do: abide in the vine.

"Abide in Me, and I in you. As the branch cannot bear fruit of itself, unless it abides in the vine, neither can you, unless you abide in Me. I am the vine, you are the branches. He who abides in Me, and I in him, bears much fruit; for without Me you can do nothing (John 15:4-5).

This is a life of rejoicing. Jesus said:

"These things I have spoken to you, that My joy may remain in you, and that your joy may be full" (John 15:11).

PUT IT IN WRITING

- Are you totally surrendered to Jesus Christ? Is there any part of your life that you are holding back?
- What are you relying on Jesus for today? What is bringing you joy?

> You can't purify the water
> by painting the pump.
>
> ADRIAN ROGERS

DAY 4

SHOW THE LOVE OF JESUS

PONDER IT

The third mark of true believers is that they **show the love of Jesus**. God is love, and when you are born again, His nature is in you.

> **He who says he is in the light, and hates his brother, is in darkness until now. He who loves his brother abides in the light, and there is no cause for stumbling in him (1 John 2:9-10).**

If His love is in you, then you will love others. If your heart is a headquarters for hate, you are not saved. You can't hate anybody, no matter what they've done. If you have any kind of racial hatred in your heart, you need to bring it to Calvary. If you hate your enemy, come to Calvary. When they were nailing Jesus to the cross, He prayed for His enemies. (See Luke 23:34.)

This is the commandment He gave His disciples after He washed their feet:

> "A new commandment I give to you, that you love one another; as I have loved you, that you also love one another" (John 13:34).

Real love is not just saying "I love you"; it is serving. Jesus washed their feet as a symbol that He was cleansing and forgiving their sin. It was steadfast love.

> ...when Jesus knew that His hour had come that He should depart from this world to the Father, having loved His own who were in the world, He loved them to the end (John 13:1).

Jesus never stopped loving His disciples. He loved old loud-mouthed Peter, the big fisherman who was rough around the edges. He loved James and John, the Sons of Thunder, with their hair-trigger tempers. Jesus loved doubting, cynical, quizzical Thomas. He loved calculating

Philip, who worried there wouldn't be enough fish. Jesus even loved Judas, who betrayed Him. Jesus washed his feet, and He said:

> **"If I then, your Lord and Teacher, have washed your feet, you also ought to wash one another's feet… By this all will know that you are My disciples, if you have love for one another" (John 13:14, 35).**

You don't have to ask what Jesus would do if He were here because He is already here. Through the Holy Spirit living in you, He is alive and well. As you abide in Him, His life comes into you and now the life you live is one that you live by faith in the Son of God who loved you and gave Himself for you. Paul said:

> **I have been crucified with Christ; it is no longer I who live, but Christ lives in me; and the life which I now live in the flesh I live by faith in the Son of God, who loved me and gave Himself for me (Galatians 2:20).**

As you abide in Christ, His life is reproduced in you. He knows what He wants to do. He can do what He wants to do because He is here. When we abide in Him, He empowers us to walk as He walked.

The mark of a true believer in Jesus Christ is not somebody who just subscribes to a code or a cause or a church; it is somebody who is abiding in Christ and who, like a branch, is drawing his life from the vine and abiding in Him.

PUT IT IN WRITING

- How has Jesus shown you His love?
- How well are you loving others? Is there anyone you hate in your heart?

> *A Christian is the visible part of the invisible Christ, and Jesus is the invisible part of the visible Christian.*
>
> ADRIAN ROGERS

DAY 5

PREACH GOD'S LOVE

▪ **PONDER IT**

Pastor Rogers told the following story:

> An evangelist named Henry Morehouse preached the love of God everywhere he went. His text was always John 3:16. A man in a little Welsh mining town named Ike Miller was a drunkard, a brawler, a profane, ungodly man. He was a gambler who consorted with prostitutes and abused and beat his wife and children.
>
> When Ike Miller heard that Henry Morehouse was holding a revival, he said, "If that preacher preaches tonight in this town, I'm going to come to the meeting. I'm going to pistol-whip him out of town." The people asked Henry Morehouse not to preach that night and to go to a different town.
>
> But Henry Morehouse said, "No, I'll be there tonight, and I'll trust God to take care of me."
>
> That night the little church was full. When this man of God stood up in the pulpit, everybody heard the back door slam. A man with a pistol in his hand walked in, sat down, and folded his arms across his chest.
>
> Henry Morehouse preached John 3:16. He poured his heart out and preached the love of God. At the close of the service, this hulking man stood up, but instead of coming forward, he turned around and left, slamming the door behind him. He walked down the street of that little mining town, and the prostitutes called to him from their upstairs windows. But he paid no attention. Some of the men in the saloon called for him to come in and have a drink. He paid no attention.
>
> He turned down a dusty side street and came to a little, weather-boarded shack. With his big, ham-like fist, he threw open the door of that shack. Inside was his wife and his little children who thought he was coming home in a drunken stupor.

The children scurried like squirrels under the bed, and his wife tried to hide the children under the bed. He looked at her and said, "Woman, you don't have to be afraid. Get the kids out from under the bed. We're gonna pray."

She said, "What?"

He said, "You heard me, woman. Get the kids. We're gonna pray." Ike Miller, his wife, and the kids kneeled by the bed and tried to pray. But he didn't know how. He said, "Oh, God," but no prayer came. He said, "Lord," but no prayer came. Then he remembered a prayer his mother had taught him when he was a boy. He prayed. "Gentle Jesus, meek and mild, look upon a little child, forgive my simplicity and suffer me to come to Thee." Ike Miller was saved at that moment.

When people asked Henry Morehouse why he didn't preach the wrath of God or preach against sin while Ike Miller sat there, he said, "Because that man needed love. He needed the love of God."

That's what our world needs. When we begin to practice what John is talking about and submit to the lordship of Jesus, when we seek the lifestyle of Jesus, when we show the love of Jesus, this world will believe that what we say is real. This is why John repeats the phrase "If we say…" It's time to stop talking the talk and start walking the walk to be like Jesus.

PUT IT IN WRITING

- How can you show God's love to those around you?
- Who in your circle of influence needs to hear about the love of God?

> If your religion hasn't changed your life, you'd better change your religion.
>
> ADRIAN ROGERS

DAY 6

A SINNER AND AN EVANGELIST

▪ PRACTICE IT

You are not saved by submitting to His lordship. You are not saved by seeking His lifestyle. You are not saved by showing His love. But if you are saved, you'll do all those things. You're saved by the grace of God.

> **Therefore, if anyone is in Christ, he is a new creation; old things have passed away; behold, all things have become new (2 Corinthians 5:17).**

The God who saved Ike Miller is the God who'll save you today. Your lifestyle may not have been the lifestyle of Ike Miller. But there's no one so good he need not be saved, and no one so bad he cannot be saved. If you want to trust Jesus, pray a prayer like this:

> *Dear Lord Jesus, Come into my heart. Forgive my sin. Look upon me, gentle Jesus, meek and mild. Look upon a little child. Forgive my simplicity and suffer me to come to Thee. Come into my heart and save me. In Jesus' Name, Amen.*

▪ PROCLAIM IT

If you prayed to receive Christ, please share your decision with another Christian you know or with your pastor. We would also like to hear about it so that we can provide you with free resources to help you grow in your new faith. Please let us know by going to **lwf.org/discover-jesus**, scrolling down the page and clicking on I BELIEVE.

Spend some time with a trusted mentor or Christian friend. Share what you have learned this week. Ask your friend if he or she sees the marks of a believer in your life. Ask God to show you where you need to grow and share the love of God with someone who needs to know about His great love.

> Our salvation deals not only
> with the sweet by-and-by but
> also with the now-and-now.
>
> ADRIAN ROGERS

Maturity is not a hundred-yard dash; it is a marathon. If you want to grow a squash, you can do that in forty days. If you want to grow an oak, you can do that in forty years.

ADRIAN ROGERS

WEEK 4

MATURITY

INTRODUCTION

Are you a growing Christian? Are you moving toward maturity? You can only be young once, but you can be immature for a long, long time. Some people who are born again cease to grow. The point is not to just become a Christian but to become a growing Christian.

> **I write to you, little children, because your sins are forgiven you for His name's sake. I write to you, fathers, because you have known Him who is from the beginning. I write to you, young men, because you have overcome the wicked one. I write to you, little children, because you have known the Father. I have written to you, fathers, because you have known Him who is from the beginning. I have written to you, young men, because you are strong, and the word of God abides in you, and you have overcome the wicked one (1 John 2:12-14).**

In the passage, there are three categories of persons—little children, young men, and fathers. John writes about growing into maturity, moving from childhood to fatherhood. We can use these age and stage markers in someone's life to gauge maturity.

Maturity is a lifelong process; nobody is born mature. You can be spiritually gifted and healthy from the moment you are saved, but you cannot be instantly mature. Our focus this week will be on how to move into maturity from childhood to adolescence to parenthood.

PRAY OVER IT

Dear God, I know You accept me and love me wherever I am in my spiritual journey. But my desire is to continually grow in You. Open my eyes this week to see where I am on my journey; open my ears to hear Your voice leading me in the direction I should go. In Jesus' Name, Amen.

DAY 1

THE THRILLING WONDERS OF CHILDHOOD

PONDER IT

The first thing a new believer experiences is salvation and forgiveness. That's the blessing of getting saved.

> **I write to you, little children, because your sins are forgiven you for His name's sake (1 John 2:12).**

Spiritual maturity is more than spiritual health. A 5-year-old can be perfectly healthy, but he's still not mature. You can have spiritual gifts and not be mature. Paul said he was limited in what he could teach the Corinthian church because of their immaturity:

> **I fed you with milk and not with solid food; for until now you were not able to receive it, and even now you are still not able; for you are still carnal (1 Corinthians 3:2-3a).**

Maturity goes beyond spirituality. If you were to receive Christ as your Lord and Savior right now, you would be immediately filled with the Holy Spirit. This does not mean that you would be a mature Christian.

> **Till we all come to the unity of the faith and of the knowledge of the Son of God, to a perfect man, to the measure of the stature of the fullness of Christ (Ephesians 4:13).**

Maturity is Christ-likeness. The word "perfect" here does not mean sinless; it means finished, or complete, wanting for nothing. This is what maturity is. The best way to measure a ministry is not in the size of buildings, amount of offering, or attendance, but in whether believers are becoming more and more like Jesus. The goal of Paul's ministry was to preach Christ so that every person who heard him would become complete and mature in Christ.

Him we preach, warning every man and teaching every man in all wisdom, that we may present every man perfect in Christ Jesus (Colossians 1:28).

The first stage of the Christian life is **the thrilling wonders of childhood.** When God blesses a family with a new baby, it brings much excitement and joy. However, babies are the most selfish, rude, and lazy creatures on Earth. If you take something away from them, they fly into a rage. They will burp in your face and just lie around the house doing nothing. Little babies are totally inconsiderate. They'll wake you up in the middle of the night and not think twice about what you need. No one looks at this stage of life and longs to go back to being a baby.

In the same way, people look at baby Christians and say they don't want to be Christians if that's the way they act. Just like babies, new Christians have their place in a family. A great family is one with grandparents, parents, teenagers, and babies, so a growing church needs believers at each point of maturity. But eventually, baby Christians have to grow up. You don't want to see 40-year-old men being rocked in the nursery. We are meant to have a childhood and then grow out of it.

Many times, when people receive Christ as children, they are mostly concerned about getting to Heaven. When new believers give their testimonies, they talk about how they got saved and how their sins are forgiven. This is wonderful, but it's only the beginning of their spiritual journeys.

PUT IT IN WRITING

- Have you accepted Christ as your Savior? What do you remember about what you thought and felt immediately after you were saved?
- How would you describe where you are currently on your spiritual journey? Have you moved out of the childhood stage?

If Jesus doesn't excite you, maybe you have calluses on your soul.

ADRIAN ROGERS

DAY 2

THE TRIUMPHANT WARFARE OF MANHOOD

PONDER IT

The second stage is **the triumphant warfare of manhood**.

> **...I write to you, young men, because you have overcome the wicked one...I have written to you, young men, because you are strong, and the word of God abides in you, and you have overcome the wicked one (1 John 2:13b-14).**

After milk bottles come mighty battles. Maturing believers move from childhood to become workers and warriors. They move past being served and look for ways to serve others. Many Christians go to church to be served. They sit in the congregation and think they've done God a wild favor. These people are saved, but they aren't in the battle. They aren't workers or warriors. They got saved and stopped growing.

When you move to the next stage, John says the Word of God has made you strong so that you can overcome the wicked one. In the average church, the devil calls the play right up the middle and goes all the way for a touchdown because a bunch of spiritual kindergartners are trying to block NFL players. Young believers are not strong, and they don't know anything about spiritual battle. Satan gets his way because he is fighting an army of spiritual children.

> **Therefore submit to God. Resist the devil and he will flee from you (James 4:7).**

Young men are strong. Believers in the adolescent stage can overcome the wicked one. Are you a victor or a victim? Are you an overcomer or are you overcome? Are you spiritually strong because the Word of God abides in you?

PUT IT IN WRITING

- Are you a worker? In what ways are you serving others?
- Are you a warrior who is a threat to Satan's kingdom? How have you overcome the wicked one in your life?

> The question isn't, "Are you afraid of the devil?". The question is, "Is the devil afraid of you?".
>
> ADRIAN ROGERS

DAY 3

THE TESTED WISDOM OF FATHERHOOD

PONDER IT

The third stage is **the tested wisdom of fatherhood.** This is the kind of spiritual maturity the Lord moves us to.

> **I write to you, fathers, because you have known Him who is from the beginning (1 John 2:13a).**

A spiritual father is a person who has come to mature wisdom because he has walked with the Lord so long that his life reflects the likeness of God. He or she knows, understands, and has moved beyond building and battling.

John is not talking about chronological age or a specific gender. This is only an illustration. If you're a woman, this applies to you. If you're a young person who has known Jesus for several years, this applies to you. You can be a spiritual father and be a teenager because he's talking about spiritual maturity.

A father is somebody who has children. Paul talked of Timothy as his son in the faith.

> **For this reason I have sent Timothy to you, who is my beloved and faithful son in the Lord, who will remind you of my ways in Christ, as I teach everywhere in every church (1 Corinthians 4:17).**

It is a great blessing to be a spiritual father or even a grandfather. When people you've won to Jesus win other people to Jesus, you get to be a spiritual grandparent. A father is known for wisdom and generosity. When you become a spiritual parent by leading others to Christ, you give your spiritual children what they need to grow in the grace and knowledge of our Lord and Savior Jesus Christ.

God is not trying to say that you substitute manhood for childlikeness. A mature adult is a composite of all of these things. No matter how old we get, we should never lose the wonder of childhood.

As we mature in our faith, we should continue to be child-like—filled with wonder and sweetness. Keep the wonder, the excitement, and the joy. Never forget what it felt like when your sins were forgiven. When you become a parent, you don't lose the wonder or step out of the warfare; all of these things help you grow in wisdom until you become a mature believer.

There ought to be a little boy in every man, and a little girl in every woman. Someone who still loves to laugh, play, and have fun. You ought to stay in the battle, and the Word of God ought to be in you. You just simply add all these things together until you become a fully mature individual—what John calls a father. Then you are at home in any crowd—with little children, young people and old people. Little children enjoy a person who is mature in the Lord if they still have their childhood and never lose the wonder. Little children loved Jesus, and they'd sit in His lap. This is what it looks like as we grow in the grace and knowledge of Jesus.

PUT IT IN WRITING

- Have you spiritually reproduced—led anyone to Christ or discipled someone? Who are your spiritual children?
- Have you lost the wonder of childhood? What do you do to care for the child inside of you?

> There are those who say that
> children make a rich man poor,
> but they have it backward.
> Children make a poor man rich.
>
> ADRIAN ROGERS

DAY 4

GROWTH REQUIRES THE MIRACLE OF LIFE

PONDER IT

We often think of sweet, old John, the beloved disciple, the disciple whom Jesus loved, the one who told us to love one another. But in his youth, John was called the Son of Thunder! He had a hair-trigger temper. His natural disposition was very selfish.

> **They said to Him, "Grant us that we may sit, one on Your right hand and the other on Your left, in Your glory" (Mark 10:37).**

> **And when His disciples James and John saw this, they said, "Lord, do You want us to command fire to come down from heaven and consume them, just as Elijah did?" But He turned and rebuked them (Luke 9:54-55a).**

John was not Mr. Nice Guy when he met Jesus, but he grew in the grace and knowledge of our Lord and Savior Jesus Christ. Later, he's called the beloved apostle. After Christ's death, he went to Samaria and led a revival. Instead of a consuming fire, he brought a Holy Ghost fire. He was trying to be first, but he taught us to sacrificially love one another. The Apostle John grew and matured. If there was hope for John, there's hope for you. You can still grow.

Growth requires the miracle of life. In order to grow, you must be born again. Give your heart to Jesus to be filled with life and the power to change. You will not be instantly mature, and there are no shortcuts. Just keep going, and you'll find that you're growing. Growth requires the passage of time.

PUT IT IN WRITING

- When did you make a decision to follow Jesus?
- When you look back at your spiritual journey, where do you see growth? How are you growing now?

> If you don't love Jesus Christ more today than you did yesterday, you're backslidden.
>
> ADRIAN ROGERS

DAY 5

GROWTH REQUIRES THE RECEIVING OF NOURISHMENT

PONDER IT

Growth requires the receiving of nourishment. We are commanded to crave the Word of God.

> **...as newborn babes, desire the pure milk of the word, that you may grow thereby (1 Peter 2:2).**

You don't give new Christians a study in Revelation. You get them in the Gospel of John. You give them the milk of the Word so that they may grow. Newborn babies are not interested in the print on the curtains or the mobile hanging over their beds. They're only interested in milk.

If your Christian walk isn't going well—if you're not winning battles or experiencing answered prayers—you should first evaluate your time in the Word. Being in Scripture only on Sunday mornings is like giving a newborn baby four gallons of milk on weekends. That's not going to lead to maturity. You must feed daily on the Word of God.

To grow, there's got to be a birth, time, and constant feeding on the Word. Little babies will put anything in their mouths. Don't be the kind of believer that consumes anything that looks like it is about God. Lots of content sounds "Christian," but some of it goes directly against the Bible. A baby believer isn't able to tell the difference, but a mature believer can. New believers will put anything in their heads. They don't understand or have discernment. You must feed on the Word of God.

PUT IT IN WRITING

- What role did the Bible play in your early life as a believer? Did you try anything that seemed "Christian" but wasn't?
- What are some habits you have developed to help you stay in God's Word and continue to grow?

> The Word of God is to your spirit
> what blood is to your body.
>
> ADRIAN ROGERS

DAY 6

DISCIPLINE AND EXERCISE

PRACTICE IT

It takes new life, time, nourishment, **discipline, and exercise** if you are to develop and not be a flabby Christian.

> **But solid food belongs to those who are of full age, that is, those who by reason of use have their senses exercised to discern both good and evil (Hebrews 5:14).**

The word for "exercise" is the word from which we get the word "gymnasium". Many Christians are spiritually flabby because they come down the aisle of the church, get baptized, and go to church every Sunday. They sit, soak, and sour because they do not exercise. If you want to be mature, get a job. Find something to do in your church. There's a place of service for you. Get busy for the Lord Jesus Christ. It is a shame and a disgrace that so many people have been Christians for so long and are still sitting in the nursery being rocked, sucking their thumbs, and crying about spilled milk.

If you're a child, thank God that you've been born into the family, but desire to become a young man. There's a battle to be fought and work to be done.

If you are a young person in Christ, you are a worker and a warrior, but desire to become a spiritual parent. Remind others of God. Become a giving person, a reproducing person. Be a person who has the knowledge of God, so that when people have problems, they can come to you. Spend so much time with God that you begin to look and act like Him.

The first step, if you haven't already done it, is being born and becoming a child of God. Do you know Jesus Christ as your personal Lord and Savior? God wants to save you, and He wants to forgive your sin. Will you pray a prayer like this?

Dear God, Thank You for loving me so much. Thank You for sending Jesus to die for my sins. Thank You for paying my sin debt and taking the judgment I deserve. You told me if I would trust You, You would save me. I trust You right now. Forgive my sin, cleanse me, make me Your child. Save me, and help me not to be ashamed of You. In Jesus' Name, Amen.

PROCLAIM IT

If you prayed to receive Christ, please share your decision with another Christian you know or with your pastor. We would also like to hear about it so that we can provide you with free resources to help you grow in your new faith. Please let us know by going to **lwf.org/discover-jesus,** scrolling down the page and clicking on I BELIEVE.

Spend time with a trusted spiritual mentor this week. Ask your mentor what fruit he or she sees in your life and how you still need to grow. Ask God to give you wisdom and to give you courage to make the changes you need to make. He wants good things for you as you grow in the grace and knowledge of your Lord and Savior, Jesus Christ.

Don't go to Heaven empty-handed.

ADRIAN ROGERS

Let go of this world, and take hold of God with both hands.

ADRIAN ROGERS

WEEK 5

THE WORLD

INTRODUCTION

Hate is an ugly word, and ugly hate is hating people who are different from you or who disagree with you. But you cannot truly love without hating some things. When you're a Christian, the Lord fills your heart with love, but you are not to love everything. Some things in this world you cannot truly love and be a child of God.

> **You who love the LORD, hate evil! He preserves the souls of His saints; He delivers them out of the hand of the wicked (Psalm 97:10).**

> **Let love be without hypocrisy. Abhor what is evil. Cling to what is good (Romans 12:9).**

You cannot love God without hating evil. You cannot cleave to that which is good without abhorring that which is evil. If you love health, then you hate disease. If you love peace, you hate war. If you love cleanliness, you hate filth. If you love people, you hate sin. If you love life, you hate death and killing.

> **Do not love the world or the things in the world. If anyone loves the world, the love of the Father is not in him (1 John 2:15).**

We're not to love the world. We have an enemy that seems friendly, and that enemy rules the world. This week, we are going to discuss the world's character, corruption, and condemnation.

PRAY OVER IT

> *Dear God, I want to hate what You hate and love what You love. I know You hate the things that hurt us and take us away from You. Help me to see the world for what it is and give me wisdom so that I can know how to live in it. In Jesus' Name, Amen.*

DAY 1

LOVE NOT THE WORLD

▇ PONDER IT

When John cautions us against loving the world, we need to understand what he meant.

John is not talking about Earth, the planet. The Bible also calls that "the world," but there's nothing wrong with loving this planet and what God has made. When God made creation, He said it was good. You can love the rocks, hills, trees, fleas, bees, and all the rest of it. He made it, and you ought to love it and enjoy it.

John is not talking about the world of people. We're to love people from every tribe and tongue without prejudice or hatred toward any person. Whether they're saved or lost, we're to love all people because God loves the people of this world.

> **For God so loved the world that He gave His only begotten Son, that whoever believes in Him shall not perish but have everlasting life (John 3:16).**

The meaning of "world" in 1 John 2:15 is the Greek word "cosmos." This word means: "a system or an order of things; a way of doing things." For instance, a cosmopolitan area is a city where people come together to work in an orderly way. A woman using cosmetics is putting her face in order.

When John says, "do not love the world," he is talking about an ungodly, devilish system that is set against Jesus Christ. Though the world, by this definition, may cozy up to you like a friend, it truly is an enemy.

PUT IT IN WRITING

- In what ways do you love and enjoy the Earth and love and enjoy the people of the world?
- Do you think of the world as an enemy or a friend? What is the difference?

> The world is the external foe.
> The flesh is the internal foe.
> The devil is the infernal foe.
>
> ADRIAN ROGERS

DAY 2

THE WORLD'S CHARACTER: A PRINCE, PHILOSOPHY, & PURPOSE

PONDER IT

There are consequences of loving and following the world. But we can't unpack that until we understand the **character of the world.**

This world has a prince: a dark, diabolical devil. This is what Jesus said about the prince of this world and his ultimate demise:

> "Now is the judgment of this world; now the ruler of this world will be cast out" (John 12:31).

> "...the ruler of this world is judged" (John 16:11).

John helps us understand that the whole world is under the influence of this prince:

> We know that we are of God, and the whole world lies under the sway of the wicked one (1 John 5:19).

Some translations say that the whole world is "in the lap" or "in the grip" of the wicked one. The whole world is being rocked and held in the hands of Satan. He is the mastermind behind this world system. He has myriads of underlings who do his bidding. He has a whole system of people working beneath him. (See Ephesians 6:12.)

This world has a philosophy: a networking of ideas and values that are skillfully woven together to entrap the most innocent.

> For the wisdom of this world is foolishness with God. For it is written, "He catches the wise in their own craftiness" (1 Corinthians 3:19).

The wisdom of the world leads to evil. Its philosophy influences everything from the schoolhouse to the statehouse. It appears in entertainment that enters our homes, in recreational theme parks, and all over the world. It may seem innocent, beautiful, or alluring, but it is all foolishness.

This world has a purpose: a calculated plan to draw you away from God. The world doesn't hate Jesus because He healed the sick or because He blessed the children. The world doesn't hate Jesus because He walked on the water or even because He died on the cross. This is what Jesus said about why the world hates Him:

"The world cannot hate you, but it hates Me because I testify of it that its works are evil" (John 7:7).

If you get right with God, the world will try to destroy you. They're not going to praise and flatter you.

Do you not know that friendship with the world is enmity with God? Whoever therefore wants to be a friend of the world makes himself an enemy of God (James 4:4b).

If you are a friend to this world that hates Jesus, you are an enemy of God. The purpose of the world is to draw your heart away from loving Jesus Christ.

"If you were of the world, the world would love its own. Yet because you are not of the world, but I chose you out of the world, therefore the world hates you" (John 15:19).

PUT IT IN WRITING
- How would you describe the philosophy of the world? How is this way of thinking influencing your community?
- How do you see the world's purpose playing out in your life or your family? In what ways are you tempted to conform to the world?
- Do you see the world's philosophy as coming from Satan? Why or why not?

DAY 3

THE WORLD'S CHARACTER: A PEOPLE

PONDER IT

Yesterday we looked at the prince, philosophy, and purpose of the world. Today we will consider the people of the world.

The world has a people. When you were saved, you came out of the world and became different. You are twice-born in a world of once-born people, and so you are going to think differently than a lot of people. What you believe starts at a different source, follows a different course, and is headed toward a different conclusion.

If you were of the world, the world would love you. But this world is not your home. You are not a part of this world system.

> **Do not love the world or the things in the world. If anyone loves the world, the love of the Father is not in him (1 John 2:15).**

The devil's goal is to squeeze you into the world's mold. The world doesn't want you to be different. It wants you to follow its prince, to believe its philosophies, to join its purpose, and to be a part of its people.

> **And do not be conformed to this world, but be transformed by the renewing of your mind, that you may prove what is that good and acceptable and perfect will of God (Romans 12:2).**

PUT IT IN WRITING

- How are Christians in your community different from people who are not saved?
- What choices have you made to live differently from the world?

> Don't get the idea that one way is the broad way and that the narrow way is a little side road going in the same direction.
>
> ADRIAN ROGERS

DAY 4

THE WORLD'S CORRUPTION: PASSIONS & POSSESSIONS

PONDER IT

We are not to love the world because of **the corruption of the world.**

> **For all that is in the world—the lust of the flesh, the lust of the eyes, and the pride of life—is not of the Father but is of the world (1 John 2:16).**

This world that tries to seduce you away from loving Jesus has three main appeals: the lust of the flesh, the lust of the eyes, and the pride of life.

Lust of the flesh: When the Bible says, "the flesh," it doesn't mean your hair, skin, or bones. But it means your old, adamic nature. The flesh is the sin nature we received from our first birth. Spirit is what we received from our second birth.

> **For the flesh lusts against the Spirit, and the Spirit against the flesh; and these are contrary to one another, so that you do not do the things that you wish (Galatians 5:17).**

When you get saved, an internal civil war begins. Your new nature wants to serve God, but the old nature doesn't want to give up and die. So, you're going to have a battle on the inside.

The Bible calls this old nature and its desires "the lust of the flesh." These desires are primarily material or physical. The lust of the flesh includes things like gluttony, laziness, drunkenness, immorality, and perversion. God has given you desires that are normal and good. A good appetite, ambition, and a healthy sex drive are gifts from God because they are part of the glue that holds the family together and makes life work. But Satan wants to take normal, God-given appetites and corrupt them.

The lust of the eyes: This deals with your possessions. The lust of the flesh deals with doing, and the lust of the eyes deals with having. This temptation may seem more refined and sophisticated than the lust of the flesh. It's the desire to want more than we need. Money is not the root of all evil, but loving it is. (See 1 Timothy 6:10.)

When you see things that you want and you think you need those things to be satisfied, that's the lust of the eyes.

The pride of life: This world says that we need to be important to have value. You need to be recognized for your achievements and get a name for yourself. You think you must be noticed.

This is why some people dress to impress or buy fancy cars. It's the reason people gossip. They think that if they put others down, they will elevate themselves. Like a drowning man in a sea of insecurity, they pull others down. That's the reason people take drugs and drink. The drunk is the life of the party and feels like somebody for a little while.

PUT IT IN WRITING

- How have you been tempted to exchange a good desire for the lust of the flesh? In what area of life is your biggest struggle?
- Is there any material possession you would not part with for the glory of God? What are you holding onto that could be keeping you from God?
- What are you relying on to give you value or position?

> I'd be a Christian if there were no Heaven or Hell, just to know the Lord Jesus Christ in this life.
>
> ADRIAN ROGERS

DAY 5

THE CONDEMNATION OF THE WORLD

PONDER IT

The system of the world deals with passions, possessions, and position. It deals with doing, and having, and being. Advertising convinces you that you are a person with discriminating tastes and above-average intelligence who likes and deserves the finer things of life. Since you feel they have described you perfectly, you buy whatever product they are selling. They know exactly how to get inside your head.

The world's system of passions, possessions, and position was in the Garden of Eden when Adam and Eve fell. Satan said the food was good to eat; he appealed to their passions—the lust of the flesh. He said it was pleasant to look at; he appealed to their desire for possession—the lust of the eyes. He said it would make them wise and give them a new position—the pride of life.

Jesus was tempted in all points like we are. While He was in the desert for 40 days and nights, the devil came to Him to tempt Him.

> **For we do not have a High Priest who cannot sympathize with our weaknesses, but was in all points tempted as we are, yet without sin (Hebrews 4:15).**

Satan tried to tempt Jesus to satisfy the lust of the flesh.

> **Now when the tempter came to Him, he said, "If You are the Son of God, command that these stones become bread" (Matthew 4:3).**

He tempted Jesus to satisfy the lust of the eyes and gain more worldly possessions.

> **Again, the devil took Him up on an exceedingly high mountain, and showed Him all the kingdoms of the world and their glory.**

> And he said to Him, "All these things I will give You if You will fall down and worship me" (Matthew 4:8-9).

He tempted Jesus to satisfy the pride of life—to get a powerful position by making a dramatic entrance onto the world stage. Be somebody important, do some magical thing, make a grand entrance.

> Then the devil took Him up into the holy city, set Him on the pinnacle of the temple, and said to Him, "If You are the Son of God, throw Yourself down" (Matthew 4:5-6a).

The devil is still working on you in the same three areas. But God wants good things for you. If you want something to do, serve God. If you want something to have, give your heart to Jesus Christ and everything else will follow. (See Matthew 5:5.) If you want to be somebody, become a child of the King. You are royalty. Why take second best? Doing, having, and being are found in Jesus Christ alone. The devil's a liar, and the world has a system that will try to draw you away from Jesus Christ.

PUT IT IN WRITING

- What really motivates you? What are your personal goals?
- Why is it important for us to know that Jesus was tempted in the same ways that we are?

> *If you're living for this world, you're painting the decks of a sinking ship.*
>
> ADRIAN ROGERS

DAY 6

THE WORLD'S CONDEMNATION

PRACTICE IT

The third reason we're not to love the world is **because of its condemnation,** where it is headed. There's one sure thing about this world system: it's not going to be here forever.

> **And the world is passing away, and the lust of it; but he who does the will of God abides forever (1 John 2:17).**

What is more important to you? The pleasures of the flesh or the joys of the Spirit? That which is seen or unseen? The praise of man or the glory of God? That which is temporal or that which is eternal? Soon the mossy fingers of decay are going to take away all the toys and trinkets you have.

You were made to serve God. If any man loves the world, it's simply because the love of the Father is not in him. The love of the Father is Jesus Christ Himself.

> **For whatever is born of God overcomes the world. And this is the victory that has overcome the world—our faith. Who is he who overcomes the world, but he who believes that Jesus is the Son of God? (1 John 5:4-5).**

If you let the love of the Father come into your heart, you'll have unspeakable joy, and you will abide forever when this Earth with its system is gone. When Madison Avenue and the moguls on Wall Street are gone, you'll be with Jesus.

You can't love Him and love the world at the same time. If you want to be saved, pray a prayer like this:

> *Dear God, I know You love me. I know You want to save me. Jesus, You died to save me, and You promised to save me if I*

would trust You. I believe You're the Son of God. I believe You paid for my sin with Your blood on the cross. I believe God raised You from the dead. Like a little child, I trust You to save me. I don't ask for a feeling or look for a sign; I stand on Your Word. You are my Lord, my Savior, my God, and my friend. Thank You for saving me. Because You died for me, I will live for You and obey You. I will not be ashamed of You, my Lord and Savior. In Jesus' Name, Amen.

PROCLAIM IT

If you prayed to receive Christ, please share your decision with another Christian you know or with your pastor. We would also like to hear about it so that we can provide you with free resources to help you grow in your new faith. Please let us know by going to **lwf.org/discover-jesus,** scrolling down the page and clicking on I BELIEVE.

Spend some time in prayer, asking God to show you the ways you have given into the lust of the flesh, the lust of the eyes, and the pride of life. When the Holy Spirit gently reveals sin to you, confess and ask God to forgive you. Then believe He has forgiven you and take the next step of faith God reveals to you. It may be reading the Bible regularly, getting more involved in your church, or sharing Christ with someone in your circle of influence.

> When you give your heart to Jesus, you're next of kin to the Holy Trinity.
>
> ADRIAN ROGERS

> One of these days, just like that, Jesus is going to come.
>
> — ADRIAN ROGERS

WEEK 6

THE END

INTRODUCTION

The sands of time are running low, and history as we know it is heading for a climax. No child of God can afford to be ignorant in these dynamic days. If we are in the last days, our lives will still be sweet with Jesus, but we must realize that the time is ripe for the appearance of a person that the Bible calls the Antichrist, a beast of a man lurking in the shadows of history.

Perilous times are here! The dynamite is in place, the fuse is laid, and the match has been struck. The days are numbered, and we need to be ready. Here are four reasons we need to be ready:

The intercession factor: We need to be praying for this world. We need to get our heads out of the clouds and get our knees on the floor.

The soul-winning factor: Instead of rearranging deck chairs on the Titanic, we need to be getting people into the lifeboats.

The family preparation factor: Living in the last days is dangerous. As parents and grandparents, we need to be putting biblical values into the hearts, minds, and lives of our children.

The comfort factor: We understand that Jesus Christ is coming again, and that fact brings us comfort.

With these four factors in mind, we are going to jump into 1 John 2 this week. We will look at what John says about the time, the tyrant, and the triumph.

PRAY OVER IT

Dear God, I see that our world is hurting, and I know that the End Times are coming. I know that the spirit of antichrist is the spirit of lying. Help me to see the truth. I want to teach my children and grandchildren so that they will be prepared. In Jesus' Name, Amen.

DAY 1

THE TIME: BE AWAKE

▪ PONDER IT

We are living in the last days, and **we need to be awake.**

> **Little children, it is the last hour; and as you have heard that the Antichrist is coming, even now many antichrists have come, by which we know that it is the last hour (1 John 2:18).**

John said this 2,000 years ago, and we are still living in the last hour. The Old Testament, the former time, was preparing for the coming of Jesus Christ. After the death, burial, resurrection, and ascension of Jesus Christ, we entered a period called "the last time." From the time that Jesus went up to Heaven until the time that Jesus is coming back, we will be in the last hour. At any time in that interval, Jesus Christ could return. All Christians, from the time of John until this time, are to be living with the expectancy that Jesus Christ may come at any moment. We are not just moving toward the last hour; we're living in it.

The Second Coming of Jesus Christ is imminent. There is no sign we're waiting for. There is no event in history we're waiting for. Jesus Christ could have come back three weeks after He ascended into Heaven. He may come back this afternoon. The Bible teaches that we are on the very edge; therefore, we should be yearning and not yawning. We should be ready for the Second Coming of the Lord Jesus Christ.

The coming of Jesus Christ is in two stages. First, the Lord Jesus Christ comes for His Church. That's the Rapture. We'll be caught up to meet the Lord in the air in a moment, in the twinkling of an eye. Then there will be the Great Tribulation here on Earth. Then Jesus Christ will come back with His saints to rule and to reign for 1,000 years. We call that the Millennium.

The Rapture has no warning signs. It could happen at any moment. Many signs precede the revelation, when Jesus Christ comes back in glory and power with His saints. At that time, He will not come for His saints; He will come with His saints.

The Bible tells of many signs that we can read just like we read signs along the road. We can tell that there is an intensity that precedes His return and warns about the coming of Christ. Not all the signs are for Christians; some of the signs are for the nation of Israel. But even if the signs are not for us, we can still read them. Coming events cast their shadows, and if Jesus Christ could've come in John's day, how much more should we be ready in these days when we see the signs?

PUT IT IN WRITING

- Do you believe that Jesus is coming again? What did you learn about His Second Coming?
- What does it look like for you to live with expectancy?

> Education is costly, but ignorance will cost you far, far more.
>
> ADRIAN ROGERS

DAY 2

WAITING FOR CHRIST'S RETURN

PONDER IT

Jesus Christ may come at any moment. This is why the Bible tells believers to wait for Him:

> ...and to wait for His Son from heaven, whom He raised from the dead, even Jesus who delivers us from the wrath to come (1 Thessalonians 1:10).

The Apostle Paul told those early Christians to wait. The word "wait" is a present infinitive, which means "to be constantly waiting." The Christians in Philippi and Corinth were to be looking for the Savior and the revelation of Jesus. He'd already come in redemption, but they were waiting for Him to come in the Rapture.

> For our citizenship is in heaven, from which we also eagerly wait for the Savior, the Lord Jesus Christ (Philippians 3:20).

> ...eagerly waiting for the revelation of our Lord Jesus Christ (1 Corinthians 1:7b).

The writer of Hebrews said:

> To those who eagerly wait for Him He will appear a second time, apart from sin, for salvation (Hebrews 9:28b).

During this time of waiting, we should be learning about, living for, longing for, and looking for His coming. We are to be expecting the Lord Jesus Christ at any moment.

> ...we should live soberly, righteously, and godly in the present age, looking for the blessed hope and glorious appearing of our great God and Savior Jesus Christ (Titus 2:12b-13).

We're not looking for some event. We're not looking for the temple to be rebuilt or looking for the Antichrist to appear. We're not looking for the regathering of Israel or earthquakes and famines. We're looking for Jesus.

PUT IT IN WRITING

- As you look at the events happening in the world, are you looking for Jesus? Where do you see Jesus at work?
- How can you stay focused on Jesus in the last hour?

> You're going to spend eternity somewhere. I've decided to spend it in the nonsmoking section.
>
> ADRIAN ROGERS

DAY 3

THE TYRANT

PONDER IT

The Antichrist is coming, and we need to be aware. The Bible describes him in many ways, but John is the only one who calls him the Antichrist.

> **Little children, it is the last hour; and as you have heard that the Antichrist is coming, even now many antichrists have come, by which we know that it is the last hour. They went out from us, but they were not of us; for if they had been of us, they would have continued with us; but they went out that they might be made manifest, that none of them were of us (1 John 2:18-19).**

He has many aliases but one wicked heart. He is also called the son of perdition, the man of sin, the wicked one, the lawless one, and the beast. Paul called him the "man of sin" and "the son of perdition":

> **Let no one deceive you by any means; for that Day will not come unless the falling away comes first, and the man of sin is revealed, the son of perdition, who opposes and exalts himself above all that is called God or that is worshiped, so that he sits as God in the temple of God, showing himself that he is God (2 Thessalonians 2:3-4).**

The Antichrist is devilish. The prefix anti- has two different meanings: "against" and "the same thing." He is the one who comes against Christ by substituting himself for Christ. He comes as the devil's messiah, a diabolical, devilish substitute. He opposes Christ and exalts himself above God.

Jesus said anyone who has seen Him has seen the Father. (See John 14:9.) The Antichrist also says the same thing. Jesus was the visible expression of the invisible God. The Antichrist will be the visible expression of the invisible devil. As Jesus is to the Father, so the

Antichrist will be to Satan. Satan desires worship. He wants people to openly worship him through his messiah, the Antichrist.

The Antichrist is divisive. John talks about other antichrists and says:

> **They went out from us, but they were not of us; for if they had been of us, they would have continued with us; but they went out that they might be made manifest, that none of them were of us (1 John 2:19).**

Some people join churches even though they've never received Jesus as their personal Savior. They may come down an aisle, be baptized, attend small groups, or join the choir. But after a while, they start to believe lies, and the Holy Spirit of God was not in them. It's not that they lost their salvation; it's that they never had it. The Bible says that in the last days people will leave the faith, and this is a fulfillment of Bible prophecy. It has not taken God by surprise.

> **Now the Spirit expressly says that in latter times some will depart from the faith, giving heed to deceiving spirits and doctrines of demons (1 Timothy 4:1).**

American evangelist D.L. Moody said, "The faith that fizzles before the finish had a flaw from the first." If they had been of us and had the Holy Spirit, they would have continued with us.

PUT IT IN WRITING

- How do you see the devilish nature of Satan at work in your community? What can you do to help others come to know Jesus?
- How can you foster unity in your church? What can you do to keep growing as a Christian so that you don't fall away?

If you are wrong about Jesus, it doesn't matter what you're right about.

ADRIAN ROGERS

DAY 4

BE AWARE

▪ PONDER IT

If we know that the Antichrist is coming, **we need to be aware** of his tactics and his character so that we can discern what is true.

The Antichrist is deceptive. The Antichrist is the master liar. He learns this from his father, the devil, who is a liar and the father of all lies. He mainly seeks to deceive people about who Jesus is. John said:

> **I have not written to you because you do not know the truth, but because you know it, and that no lie is of the truth. Who is a liar but he who denies that Jesus is the Christ? He is antichrist who denies the Father and the Son. Whoever denies the Son does not have the Father either; he who acknowledges the Son has the Father also.**
>
> **These things I have written to you concerning those who try to deceive you (1 John 2:21-23, 26).**

John gives believers this word of caution:

> **Beloved, do not believe every spirit, but test the spirits, whether they are of God; because many false prophets have gone out into the world. By this you know the Spirit of God: Every spirit that confesses that Jesus Christ has come in the flesh is of God, and every spirit that does not confess that Jesus Christ has come in the flesh is not of God. And this is the spirit of the Antichrist, which you have heard was coming, and is now already in the world (1 John 4:1-3).**

> **For many deceivers have gone out into the world who do not confess Jesus Christ as coming in the flesh. This is a deceiver and an antichrist...If anyone comes to you and does not bring this doctrine, do not receive him into your house nor greet**

him; for he who greets him shares in his evil deeds (2 John 7, 10-11).

If somebody comes to your door to give you religious literature or invite you to a church, find out what they believe about Jesus Christ. Do they believe that Jesus Christ is the Son of God, co-equal, co-eternal, with Almighty God? If they don't, they're not headed to Heaven. The spirit of antichrist is already in the world.

The Antichrist is destructive. If you don't abide with Christ, you're going to miss eternal life, and you're going to miss Jesus.

And this is the promise that He has promised us—eternal life (1 John 2:25).

Everlasting life doesn't mean eternal existence; you already have that. When God made you, God breathed into your nostrils the breath of life, and you became a living soul. You could no more cease to exist than God Himself could cease to exist. Your soul will be in existence somewhere when the sun, moon, and stars have grown cold. You have everlasting existence. What you need is everlasting life. You're going to spend eternity somewhere: Heaven or Hell.

Many antichrists shall come, and John tells us to be awake! He speaks of the tyrant, the Antichrist who is coming, so that we can be aware!

PUT IT IN WRITING

- What are some cults you know of in your community? How can you discern what is true?
- Do you know for sure that you will spend eternity in Heaven? What is keeping you or others in your community from following Jesus?

> Anything anybody can talk you into, somebody else can talk you out of.
>
> ADRIAN ROGERS

DAY 5

THE TRIUMPH: ABIDE

◼ PONDER IT

Then John speaks of the triumph. Our Lord is on His way, and **we need to be awake, aware, and abiding.**

> **Therefore let that *abide* in you which you heard from the beginning. If what you heard from the beginning *abides* in you, you also will *abide* in the Son and in the Father...But the anointing which you have received from Him *abides* in you, and you do not need that anyone teach you; but as the same anointing teaches you concerning all things, and is true, and is not a lie, and just as it has taught you, you will *abide* in Him. And now, little children, *abide* in Him, that when He appears, we may have confidence and not be ashamed before Him at His coming. If you know that He is righteous, you know that everyone who practices righteousness is born of Him (1 John 2:24, 27-29, emphasis added).**

Abide in the Word of God: The word "abide" means "to settle down, to be at home, to remain." Let the Word of God be at home in you. Learn to appreciate and apply the Word of God. The way you know the Father and the Son is through the Word of God.

Abide in the Spirit of God: In the Old Testament, when they were getting a prophet, a priest, or a king ready for service, they would pour oil on him. It was called an anointing because that oil was a symbol of the Holy Spirit. In the New Testament, we are the prophets, priests, and kings, and we have been anointed with the Holy Spirit. When we get saved, the Holy Spirit comes to abide in us.

Bible teachers and personal study are good, but you would never know anything apart from the Holy Spirit. The Holy Spirit of God is the One who teaches you. Jesus said:

> "But the Helper, the Holy Spirit, whom the Father will send in My name, He will teach you all things, and bring to your remembrance all things that I said to you" (John 14:26).

You need to abide in the Holy Spirit so He can teach you in these last days. The Holy Spirit of God in our hearts is there to affirm the truth. The Word of God and the Spirit of God will teach you the truth.

Abide in the Son of God: Abide in Jesus Christ. If the Word of God abides in you and you abide in it, then you will abide in the Son. If the Spirit of God abides in you and you abide in Him, then the Son of God is going to be revealed in you. You will be at home with Jesus, and Jesus will be at home with you.

The early Christians had a word, "maranatha," that means, "even so, come, Lord Jesus." We want Him to come, and we long for His return. We want to go home to be with the Lord Jesus, not because we are sick of this world, but because our hearts beat with anticipation for the coming of our Lord and Savior. You can meet Him with confidence.

PUT IT IN WRITING

- How do you abide in the Word of God? What are your routines or habits that help you stay connected to His Word?
- How has the Holy Spirit helped you discern the truth on your spiritual journey? How do you think you will react when you see Jesus?

The Spirit of God applies the Word of God, and both go together to reveal the Son of God.

ADRIAN ROGERS

DAY 6

MEET CHRIST WITH BOLDNESS AND JOY

PRACTICE IT

Pastor Rogers told this story:

> When I was a little boy, my dad was in the Coast Guard, and he drove a Model A Ford. Before he went off to duty, he would tell my brother and me what we needed to do while he was gone. We had yard work to do and chores. We knew that when Dad came home, we had to report. I must confess, I was not always very diligent in doing everything that my father told me to do.
>
> But a Model A Ford has a peculiar sound. I could hear my dad's Model A Ford coming into our neighborhood. If I was playing outside and saw that black Model A Ford coming, I would run after it and try to step onto the running board of the car to ride the rest of the way home.
>
> If I had done what my dad told me to do, I'd just run and jump on the running board, reach in the window, hug his neck, and kiss him. It was such a joy to see him. But other times when I heard that Model A Ford coming, I'd go the other way because I had not been abiding. I had not been obeying and doing what he'd told me to do. Now he's my father either way, so he loved me either way.
>
> I'm going to meet Jesus someday, and when He comes, I want to meet Him with boldness. I want to meet Him with joy because I am abiding in Him and doing what He asked me to do.

What is the difference between Christ and the Antichrist? The Antichrist is going to turn this world into a concentration camp and give everybody a number. Jesus calls His sheep by name. So, the big question is: When He comes, will your name be called, or will your number be up? Do you know Jesus?

Be awake! The Antichrist is coming. Be aware! Our Lord is on His way. Be abiding in the Word of God and in the Spirit of God. Abide in the Son of God, so that when He appears you'll have confidence and not be ashamed at His coming.

If you want to be saved, pray a prayer like this:

Dear God, I need You. My sin deserves judgment, but I need mercy. I want to be saved. Help me today. With all my heart I trust in You. Forgive my sin; I turn from it now. I accept You as Lord and want Your will for my life. Make me Your child. In Jesus' Name, Amen.

PROCLAIM IT

If you prayed to receive Christ, please share your decision with another Christian you know or with your pastor. We would also like to hear about it so that we can provide you with free resources to help you grow in your new faith. Please let us know by going to **lwf.org/discover-jesus**, scrolling down the page and clicking on I BELIEVE.

Spend some time considering whether you are ready for Christ's return and how you can help your children get ready. We are already in the last days, and Jesus is coming at any moment. Ask God how He wants you to live and ask Him to show you how to abide in Him. Ask Him to give you an opportunity to join His work and share Christ with someone in your circle of influence.

> **If you're living for this world only, all you're doing is rearranging the deck chairs on the Titanic.**
>
> ADRIAN ROGERS

> A rich man is poor, a strong man is weak, and an educated man is ignorant until he comes to know the Lord Jesus Christ. Without Jesus, there is no hope.
>
> ADRIAN ROGERS

WEEK 7

HEAVEN

INTRODUCTION

Many people are living lives of quiet desperation. But we do not live without hope. Fellowship with Jesus Christ is sweeter than any other. Without this fellowship, life is not so sweet. To know Jesus is to know eternal, abundant life. Jesus said:

> "I have come that they may have life, and that they may have it more abundantly" (John 10:10b).

Without Jesus, nothing makes sense. Man is ignorant of his past and afraid of his future, so he's somewhere in between mystery and misery. But if you know the Lord Jesus Christ, you have the sweetest fellowship on this side of Heaven. If that's true, imagine the fellowship you will have on the other side of Heaven.

> **Behold what manner of love the Father has bestowed on us, that we should be called children of God! Therefore the world does not know us, because it did not know Him. Beloved, now we are children of God; and it has not yet been revealed what we shall be, but we know that when He is revealed, we shall be like Him, for we shall see Him as He is. (1 John 3:1-2).**

In light of this truth, we need to learn about three things: the Christian's dignity, the Christian's destiny, and the Christian's duty.

PRAY OVER IT

Dear God, I confess that sometimes I lose hope and get discouraged. I long for the full and abundant life You promised. Help me to understand the depth of Your love for me and how I should live in light of all You have revealed to us. In Jesus' Name, Amen.

DAY 1

DIGNITY: WHAT WE ARE

PONDER IT

We need to have the **Christian's dignity.** We are children of God, sons and daughters of glory, Christ's brothers and sisters.

> **Behold what manner of love the Father has bestowed on us, that we should be called children of God! (1 John 3:1).**

> **...for whom are all things and by whom are all things, in bringing many sons to glory... (Hebrews 2:10b).**

Christ is in you, and you are in Him. You are united with Jesus Christ.

> **For both He who sanctifies and those who are being sanctified are all of one, for which reason He is not ashamed to call them brethren, saying: "I will declare Your name to My brethren" (Hebrews 2:11-12a).**

As the collective Church, we are partakers of the divine nature of Jesus Christ. He has our nature because He took human nature, and we have His nature because we have been born of God. Jesus prayed His highest priestly prayer when He prayed:

> **"And the glory which You gave Me I have given them, that they may be one just as We are one: I in them, and You in Me; that they may be made perfect in one, and that the world may know that You have sent Me, and have loved them as You have loved Me" (John 17:22-23).**

There is nothing you can do to make God love you any more than He already loves you. He loves you as much as He loves His own Son. Jesus prayed that we would know how much God loves us.

PUT IT IN WRITING

- What does it mean to you that you are considered a child of God?
- What parts of Jesus' identity do we also share before God? How do we partake in His divine nature?

> You may think that God has forgotten you, but He hasn't and never will.
>
> ADRIAN ROGERS

DAY 2

OUR FATHER

▪ PONDER IT

Jesus is the firstborn Son, but He is the firstborn in a family of many brothers and sisters. We are literally the brothers and sisters of Jesus and the sons and daughters of God. Romans 8 says:

> **For whom He foreknew, He also predestined to be conformed to the image of His Son, that He might be the firstborn among many brethren (Romans 8:29).**

> **For you did not receive the spirit of bondage again to fear, but you received the Spirit of adoption by whom we cry out, "Abba, Father" (Romans 8:15).**

"Abba Father" means "Daddy Father" in Aramaic. We can speak to God and call Him, "Daddy" or "Papa."

You have the Father's care. We are not beggars or orphans. Our Father is obligated to take care of us. This is why we have no reason to worry.

> **Look at the birds of the air, for they neither sow nor reap nor gather into barns; yet your heavenly Father feeds them. Are you not of more value than they? (Matthew 6:26).**

You have the Father's correction. God allows us to go through trouble at times because God loves us. At times, God even engineers our trouble:

> **And you have forgotten the exhortation which speaks to you as to sons: "My son, do not despise the chastening of the Lord, nor be discouraged when you are rebuked by Him; for whom the Lord loves He chastens, and scourges every son whom He receives." If you endure chastening, God deals with you**

as with sons; for what son is there whom a father does not chasten? (Hebrews 12:5-7).

Your own parents disciplined you because they loved you, even if it was hard for them to watch you suffer. In the same way, God disciplines and teaches those He loves.

When a little boy comes to his front door covered in mud from head to toe, his dad probably won't let him inside the house. First, his dad will hose him off in the yard. It's not because the father rejects the son, but because he rejects the mud. Sometimes God must hose off the mud in our lives.

You have the Father's compassion. His heart is broken when your heart is broken. It should be easy to talk to Him.

As a father pities his children, so the LORD pities those who fear Him (Psalm 103:13).

Though He is Judge and Ruler, He is also your good Father.

And because you are sons, God has sent forth the Spirit of His Son into your hearts, crying out, "Abba, Father!" (Galatians 4:6).

You have the Father's companionship. You are never alone, and He is never too busy to talk to you. We are a part of the family of God. Your Father is watching over you. You may think you're alone, but you're not alone. We are sons and daughters of God.

PUT IT IN WRITING

- Is it easy or difficult for you to think of God as your Father? Why is that?
- Do you interact with God like He is your Father or like He is your ruler and judge? How does seeing Him as a Father change your perspective?

> It is better to have a father who owns a bakery than to have a loaf of bread.
>
> ADRIAN ROGERS

DAY 3

DESTINY: WHAT WE WILL BE

PONDER IT

Not only do you see our dignity and what we are, but notice the **Christian's destiny** and what we will be:

> **Beloved, now we are children of God; and it has not yet been revealed what we shall be, but we know that when He is revealed, we shall be like Him, for we shall see Him as He is (1 John 3:2).**

Some things we don't know and aren't supposed to know because they haven't been revealed to us. Many things about the future are kept from us on purpose. Jesus said:

> **"I still have many things to say to you, but you cannot bear them now" (John 16:12)**

> **"But you, Daniel, shut up the words, and seal the book until the time of the end; many shall run to and fro, and knowledge shall increase" (Daniel 12:4).**

There are a lot of things we don't know: What are we going to be like when we get to Heaven? What are we going to look like? What age will we be? What will we eat? Don't even try to answer those questions.

A 4-year-old can ask questions nobody can answer except God. Don't try to explain everything about what we're going to be like in our resurrection bodies. There are some things we can't be dogmatic about, but there's something we can be bull-dogmatic about: we will be like Jesus, and that's good enough.

PUT IT IN WRITING

- What are some questions you have or have been asked about the Christian faith that you don't know how to answer?
- How do you feel about not knowing some things and living with unanswered questions?

> If you tell people that you don't know when you don't know, then maybe they'll believe you when you tell them you do know when you do know.
>
> ADRIAN ROGERS

DAY 4

DESTINY: WE WILL SEE HIM AND BE LIKE HIM

PONDER IT

Even though there are a lot of things we don't know about Christ's return and Heaven, there are three things we can be certain of.

> **Beloved, now we are children of God; and it has not yet been revealed what we shall be, but we know that when He is revealed, we shall be like Him, for we shall see Him as He is (1 John 3:2).**

Christ is going to appear. Jesus Christ is coming back to this Earth. We know the stories about His life on Earth from the four Gospels. But we are waiting for His Second Coming. Jesus went to glory, and He's coming back in glory. He appeared once, and He is coming back to physically appear on this Earth.

We will see Him for who He truly is. When He was here in His humanity, He wore a crown of thorns and died with criminals. But when He comes again, we will see Him in His glory.

Before God hurled this planet out into space, before God flung out the sun, moon, and stars, before God scooped out the oceans and heaped out the mountains and dotted the hillsides with flowers, and before God breathed into Man's nostrils the breath of life, Jesus was there with the Father in a glorified state. After coming into a world of woe, His work was finished, and He was glorified with the Father in Heaven again.

> **"And now, O Father, glorify Me together with Yourself, with the glory which I had with You before the world was" (John 17:5).**

Those who go to Heaven get to behold the glory of Jesus Christ. One day, Jesus will appear, and we will see Him as He is.

We will be like Him. John linked being "like Him" and "seeing Him" together. His presence is so powerful that if you saw Him now in your human flesh, you would disintegrate.

> ...**He who is the blessed and only Potentate, the King of kings and Lord of lords, who alone has immortality, dwelling in unapproachable light, whom no man has seen or can see, to whom be honor and everlasting power. Amen (1 Timothy 6:15b-16).**

Jesus dwells in such glory that we cannot even approach it. Jesus dwells in light that is more powerful than the sun. If we were not made like Him, our eyes could not stand the sight. But we are going to be like Him, and we're going to see Him as He is.

> **As for me, I will see Your face in righteousness; I shall be satisfied when I awake in Your likeness (Psalm 17:15).**

It is certain that Jesus will appear; we will see Him; we will be like Him. We may not know what we will physically look like, but we know we will be fully satisfied.

PUT IT IN WRITING

- What are you looking forward to in Heaven when you see Jesus and will be like Him?
- Who are you taking to Heaven with you? Who are the people you want to bring to Jesus so that they can know Him too?

> Christ is standing in the wings,
> getting ready to step back on
> the stage of human history.
>
> ADRIAN ROGERS

DAY 5

DUTY: WHAT WE SHOULD BE

PONDER IT

We know our Christian dignity and destiny, so now, we need to know our **Christian duty.**

> **And everyone who has this hope in Him purifies himself, just as He is pure (1 John 3:3).**

We need to hope for His coming. In the Bible, "hope" means absolute certainty mixed with anticipation. The coming of Jesus is a divine certainty mingled with excited anticipation.

When children sit in the backseat of a car on the way to a beach vacation, they excitedly ask, "Are we there yet?" many times. With the same anticipation, we must look forward with longing and readiness to see Jesus come again.

We must prepare ourselves for His coming. John said we must purify ourselves.

> **And now, little children, abide in Him, that when He appears, we may have confidence and not be ashamed before Him at His coming (1 John 2:28).**

Your heart needs to be pure, not a headquarters for hate. If you have grudges, worldly habits, or unrighteous thoughts, you need to cut them out of your life as if Jesus Christ were coming back this afternoon. You need to live with purity because He could come back at any time.

> **Therefore, having these promises, beloved, let us cleanse ourselves from all filthiness of the flesh and spirit, perfecting holiness in the fear of God (2 Corinthians 7:1).**

You might want to live your life your own way and just hope you make it to Heaven. But that won't satisfy God, and it won't satisfy you. You shouldn't get saved and live a holy life because you are afraid of what God will do to you if you don't. You live a pure life so that when you pray, nothing keeps your soul from your Savior.

Some teenagers were out one night, and one of them suggested they vandalize a building. A godly girl in that crowd said she didn't want to do that. One of them began to tease her and said she was afraid that her daddy would hurt her. She said, "No, I'm afraid I'd hurt my daddy."

That's the difference between law and love. Those who have the hope of the Second Coming of Jesus Christ in their hearts should want to be pure when He comes again. We are to be looking for His coming, living for His coming, and longing for His coming.

Some people say Jesus can come back after they get married or after they buy a house or after they are successful. Paul said:

For to me, to live is Christ, and to die is gain (Philippians 1:21).

PUT IT IN WRITING

- Are you afraid of hurting your heavenly Father and breaking His heart when you sin? How does this change your perspective on how you ought to live?
- How is your hope of Jesus' return purifying your life? How are the decisions and choices you make different because you believe Jesus is coming back?

> The best thing that could happen to anyone is for Jesus Christ to come right now. Eternity with Christ will be better than any earthly pleasure.
>
> ADRIAN ROGERS

DAY 6

THE RETURN

▪ PRACTICE IT

Decades ago, a little boy asked his mother if she could think of the happiest day of her life. As they sat on the front porch, his mother rocked in the porch swing and smiled as she put down her knitting needles. He thought that surely she would recount the time his father proposed to her on their farm or maybe the day he professed his love to her.

But instead, she replied, "Back when I was a little girl, my Daddy went to fight in the Civil War with all the other men in town. All the women and children worked hard every day, and times were very tough. One morning, we received word that Daddy was killed in battle. Mama put on a smile during the day, but at night when she thought we went to bed, she would weep and cry out to God."

"You asked me about the happiest day of my life," she said, "I'll tell you about it. Months after we heard my Daddy had passed away, Mother was sitting on the porch, very much like we are, snapping beans. She saw a man coming down the road. She threw those beans in the air and said, 'That's your Daddy!' and we ran as fast as we could across that field to embrace him."

Even your finest day will pale into insignificance to the day when you see Him and your eyes behold the King. Our dignity is that we are the sons and daughters of God. Our destiny is that we will be like Jesus. Our duty is to be pure, ready for the day He comes again.

The only way to be a son or daughter of God is to be born into His family.

But as many as received Him, to them He gave the right to become children of God, to those who believe in His name (John 1:12).

If you died today, you need to know you would be with Jesus. If you are not saved and want to be saved, pray a prayer like this:

Dear God, My sin deserves judgment, but I need mercy. I'm lost, and I need to be saved. I'm tired of just good intentions. I'm tired of just plain religion. I want to know You. I need to be saved. Jesus, You died for me. Thank You for dying for my sins. I now receive You by faith as my Lord and Savior. Come into my heart and take control of my life. I turn it all over to You. I will follow You and live for You all the days of my life, not in order to be saved, but because You've saved me. Thank You for saving me. I receive it by faith right now. Give me the courage to make it public and not to be ashamed of You. In Jesus' Name, Amen.

PROCLAIM IT

If you prayed to receive Christ, please share your decision with another Christian you know or with your pastor. We would also like to hear about it so that we can provide you with free resources to help you grow in your new faith. Please let us know by going to **lwf.org/discover-jesus,** scrolling down the page and clicking on I BELIEVE.

Pray for those in your circle of influence who do not know Jesus as their Lord and Savior. Ask God to give you an opportunity to share with them what you know about Jesus.

> The One who opened to you
> the doors of grace will open
> to you the doors of glory.
>
> ADRIAN ROGERS

The devil's a great counterfeiter. He'd just as soon send you to Hell from the pew as from the gutter.

ADRIAN ROGERS

WEEK 8

SALVATION

INTRODUCTION

Many people misunderstand true salvation. They have culture, but they don't have Calvary. They have religion, but they don't have righteousness. The devil wants you to be satisfied with a form of religion without genuine and real salvation.

John gives us clarity on real salvation. This passage is a warning so that you won't be deceived and miss the whole thing.

> **Whoever commits sin also commits lawlessness, and sin is lawlessness. And you know that He was manifested to take away our sins, and in Him there is no sin. Whoever abides in Him does not sin. Whoever sins has neither seen Him nor known Him. Little children, let no one deceive you. He who practices righteousness is righteous, just as He is righteous. He who sins is of the devil, for the devil has sinned from the beginning. For this purpose the Son of God was manifested, that He might destroy the works of the devil. Whoever has been born of God does not sin, for His seed remains in him; and he cannot sin, because he has been born of God (1 John 3:4-9).**

This passage shows the rebellion that proves our sinfulness, the righteousness that proclaims our sonship, and the redemption that proves our salvation.

PRAY OVER IT

Dear God, I confess that I sometimes wonder if I am experiencing the abundant Christian life. I wonder if I'm doing enough or believing the right things. Open my eyes this week to see what You have for me and help me to understand what it means to truly be saved. In Jesus' Name, Amen.

DAY 1

THE REBELLION THAT PROVES OUR SINFULNESS

PONDER IT

We sit in churches, well-dressed with benign smiles on our faces, but God looks into our hearts and sees the rebellion that is there.

> **Whoever commits sin also commits lawlessness, and sin is lawlessness (1 John 3:4).**

This is perhaps the clearest and the best definition of sin in the Bible. Sin is breaking God's law.

> **Therefore, to him who knows to do good and does not do it, to him it is sin (James 4:17).**

> **All unrighteousness is sin, and there is sin not leading to death (1 John 5:17).**

These verses give definitions of sin, but the most concise definition of sin is the transgression of the Law. Sin is lawlessness.

God created the whole Universe and built laws into this Universe: physical laws and moral laws. The whole Universe works according to the fixed laws of God. God gave laws to establish order. God made the stars to move in their orbits. God made the tides to ebb and flow. God made your body to work according to certain principles. These are built into nature and into the moral system of things. There are material and moral laws that bring order to the world.

The natural and moral laws are for our welfare. If we didn't have the law of gravity, we would float off the planet and into space. In the same way, moral law is for our welfare. God doesn't need anything **from** us; He already has everything. God made these laws **for** us. Sin is the transgression of the Law, and when we transgress, we break God's law and God's heart because He loves us.

Lawlessness is **the rebellion that proves our sinfulness.** We look at people who have open defiance and disrespect for the Law, and we call them outlaws. But all of us are outlaws because the Bible says sin is the transgression of the Law and all have sinned (See Romans 3:23.) No one can say he has never broken one of God's Ten Commandments.

You may think you haven't sinned very much or that your small transgression is not as bad as others. But if you have ever taken anything that didn't belong to you, whether it was a nickel off your mother's dresser or a toy out of your neighbor's yard or an answer in school when you cheated, you have sinned. If you have ever told a lie at least one time, whether it was a white lie or in technicolor, you have sinned. People are not liars because they tell lies; they tell lies because they are liars. People are not thieves because they steal; they steal because they are thieves. The problem is in the human heart!

Sin lurks in every human heart. The Bible says:

The heart is deceitful above all things, and desperately wicked; who can know it? (Jeremiah 17:9).

Even if your heart tries to deceive you into thinking you are righteous, you are a sinner. Your rebellion proves your sinfulness.

PUT IT IN WRITING

- How does it change your perspective to think of God's laws as being there for your good?
- Have you ever stolen something or told a lie? Do you see yourself as a liar and a thief?

> Every time God says, "Thou shalt not," He's saying, "Don't hurt yourself." Every time God says, "Thou shalt," God is saying, "Help yourself to happiness."
>
> ADRIAN ROGERS

DAY 2

THE RIGHTEOUSNESS THAT PROCLAIMS OUR SONSHIP

PONDER IT

Secondly, we have **the righteousness that proclaims our sonship.** John began this section by reminding us that we are children of God.

> **Beloved, now we are children of God; and it has not yet been revealed what we shall be, but we know that when He is revealed, we shall be like Him, for we shall see Him as He is (1 John 3:2).**

When you accept Jesus, you have the righteousness that proclaims your sonship.

> **And you know that He was manifested to take away our sins, and in Him there is no sin. Whoever abides in Him does not sin (1 John 3:5).**

Now, if we're in Christ, if we're saved, the Bible says we are not going to sin. We have a lot of people who say they're on the way to Heaven, but there's been no change in their life—none at all. They could be called baptized pagans because there's no change. The Bible says anyone who is in Christ is a new creation (See 2 Corinthians 5:17.)

To be clear, you're not saved by reforming your life. Our Lord never tells us to clean up our lives in order to be saved. That's backward. We come to Jesus just as we are, but Jesus did not come to save us in our sin so we could keep sinning. He came to save us from our sin. If we belong to Him, we're going to be like Him.

> **Little children, let no one deceive you. He who practices righteousness is righteous, just as He is righteous (1 John 3:7).**

If you're not righteous, you're not saved. The word "Christian" means "Christlike," and in Christ there's no sin. You can't be Christlike and live a life of sin.

This brings a real problem because all of us know that we fail as Christians. This is not talking about sinless perfection. Nobody is sinlessly perfect. If you study the lives of the saints, you will find out that they sinned. For example, Abraham lied about his wife, Moses lost his temper, Peter denied the Lord, and David was unfaithful to his wife. The Bible shows their faults and their failures, yet this passage of Scripture says that if we abide in Jesus we will not sin.

The word for "abide" in the Greek language is in the present continuous tense. The New International Version reflects this verb tense: "No one who lives in him keeps on sinning." The New American Standard says, "No one who remains in Him sins continually." It doesn't mean that you cannot slip and fall or that you are unable to sin. If it meant that, then John would have to contradict himself. Earlier in this epistle, he said:

If we say that we have not sinned, we make Him a liar, and His word is not in us (1 John 1:10).

John is saying that when you give your heart to the Lord Jesus Christ, there is a change, a radical dramatic change. Because you're saved and have the nature of God in you, your life is changed. You do not habitually practice sin.

PUT IT IN WRITING

- What are the benefits of being a son or daughter of God? How does receiving the righteousness of Christ change your identity?
- How has your life changed after you made Jesus the Lord of your life? Is sinning a habitual part of your lifestyle?

> What we need to do is to take the policeman off the street corner and put the policeman in the heart.
>
> ADRIAN ROGERS

DAY 3

KEEPING THE COMMANDMENTS

PONDER IT

The goal is not to be sinlessly perfect, but to not live in a lifestyle of sin. God's desire for us is that we don't sin. If we do slip and fall, Jesus Christ is there.

> **My little children, these things I write to you, so that you may not sin. And if anyone sins, we have an Advocate with the Father, Jesus Christ the righteous. He is the atoning sacrifice for our sins, and not only for ours but also for the sins of the whole world (1 John 2:1-2).**

"Advocate" is just a fancy word for "lawyer." We have someone who's going to plead our case before Heaven.

> **Now by this we know that we know Him if we keep His commandments. He who says, "I know Him," and does not keep His commandments, is a liar, and the truth is not in him (1 John 2:3-4).**

If you are not trying to keep the commands of Jesus, then you do not know Him. The word "keep" is a navigational word sailors used. They didn't have radar or global positioning satellites to keep them on track as they crossed the sea. They steered by keeping to the stars. Those stars are fixed in Heaven, just like God's laws are fixed. The sailors put their eyes on the stars and steered by the stars. They called it "keeping" the stars. A sailor could get blown off course, and in a time of distraction, misturn the wheel, but he had a guide for his journey and a direction he was going. Keeping the stars gave him a fixed standard he sailed by.

The Bible says if we know Jesus, we are going to keep His commandments and steer our lives by God's stars. We're going to keep His Word. If you do not care for God's commandments, if you're living your life by your own rules and doing as you please, you don't know Him. If you don't care about God's commandments, if you are not steering by God's stars, if you are habitually practicing sin, you don't know Him. You're not saved.

Many people have an easy "believism," where they say they believe in Jesus and that He died for their sins, but they have not bowed their knee to Jesus Christ to make Him the Lord of their lives. True salvation is more than saying you believe; it's an act of faith that creates a change. If religion has not changed your life, you don't have the Bible kind of religion.

Many people have joined churches who have never met Jesus. They have never really been saved, and their rebellion proves their sinfulness. We can have the righteousness that proclaims our sonship by believing in Jesus Christ as Savior and Lord.

PUT IT IN WRITING

- How are you doing at keeping God's Word? In what ways are you using the Bible to guide your life?
- Is Jesus Christ the Lord of your life? What does it mean to you that Jesus is your Savior and Lord?

> The reason that many people are still living in sin, even with their names on church rolls, is that they've met creeds, but they've not met Christ.
>
> ADRIAN ROGERS

DAY 4

THE REDEMPTION THAT PROVIDES OUR SALVATION

PONDER IT

We have **the redemption that provides our salvation.** When God tells us how to live, it doesn't mean we can do it on our own, apart from the power of the Holy Spirit. What about the sins we committed before we were saved? The Good News is that Jesus was revealed to take away our sins.

> **And you know that He was manifested to take away our sins, and in Him there is no sin (1 John 3:5).**

In Leviticus 16, God gave the Israelites the ritual of the scapegoat. The high priest took two goats to represent the people. He laid his hand on the head of one of the goats and confessed the sins of the people. He symbolically placed their sins on the goat. Then that goat would be killed because the punishment for sin is death. The high priests would take the other goat, the scapegoat, and lead it away into the wilderness and release it—never to return. The goat was a picture of Jesus Christ. Our sins were laid upon Him, and He died on the cross for our sins. He buried our sins in the grave of God's forgetfulness, never to be brought up against us again.

We are redeemed from the penalty of sin. Jesus gave Himself as the atoning sacrifice for all our sins. When John the Baptist saw Him, he said:

> **"Behold! The Lamb of God who takes away the sin of the world!" (John 1:29b).**

We are redeemed from the power of Satan. Jesus came to destroy the power of the devil. If you're still living like the devil, it's because you belong to the devil.

He who sins is of the devil, for the devil has sinned from the beginning. For this purpose the Son of God was manifested, that He might destroy the works of the devil (1 John 3:8).

Sometimes we criticize Hollywood and non-Christians because of the bad things they do. But they're sinners. The problem in many churches is that we don't teach people how to be saved. We get them involved in the church and think our job is done. But rather than being a sheepfold, the church becomes a zoo. The pastor tries to teach people not to do what they naturally do. But unless they are redeemed, they will continue to sin.

The word "destroy" does not mean "annihilate" in the Greek language; it means "to make ineffective." Jesus put Satan out of commission. On the cross, Jesus ruined Satan's kingdom, and he has no power or authority over you. Before you were saved, you were Satan's pawn. You thought you were free to do what you wanted, but you were not. You were Satan's slave, but Jesus came to set you free.

Jesus came to destroy the destroyer, and because you have new life in Jesus Christ, you will never ever face the penalty of your sin. You can tell Satan to go away because you don't have to listen to him. You don't have to obey him because his power is broken. If you don't understand that, you're going to struggle to live the Christian life.

PUT IT IN WRITING

- How have you seen Jesus break the power of sin in your life?
- Is your church teaching sinners not to sin or leading people to Jesus? What is the difference?

> Without law, there is no order, and without law, rather than having a cosmos, you have chaos.
>
> ADRIAN ROGERS

DAY 5

REDEEMED FROM THE PRINCIPLE OF SELF

PONDER IT

We are redeemed from the principle of self. If Jesus just dealt with your sin, you would still have to deal with your sin nature. But Jesus redeemed you from the principle of self.

> **Whoever has been born of God does not sin, for His seed remains in him; and he cannot sin, because he has been born of God (1 John 3:9).**

When you get saved or are born again, **you get a new dynamic.** When you were born the first time, you had physical life. When you received Jesus as your personal Savior, you received spiritual life. (See John 3:6.) Everybody has had a fleshly birth, but not everybody has had a spiritual birth.

The Word of God is your spiritual Father, and the Holy Spirit quickens and gives you life. You become a new person. When you become a new person, you have a new life, a new dynamic. You are no longer dependent upon your own efforts to live a better life.

Because you have a new dynamic, **you have a new desire.** Your Father's seed is in you. When you were saved, you were born again, not of corruptible seed, but of incorruptible seed.

> **...having been born again, not of corruptible seed but incorruptible, through the word of God which lives and abides forever (1 Peter 1:23).**

A divine life principle is in you and that gives you a new desire. The Amplified Bible says, "God's nature abides in him." God's nature is holiness and righteousness.

> **Little children, let no one deceive you. He who practices righteousness is righteous, just as He is righteous (1 John 3:7).**

Once you get saved, you can never be unsaved any more than you can be unborn. When you were born physically, that was settled. When you were born again, that was settled for eternity. You can't be unborn physically or spiritually.

Some people think that when you get saved, you get to sin all you want. But what changes when you are truly saved is that you don't want to sin. When you get a new dynamic, you get a new desire.

If you don't have that desire, you'd better check up on your salvation. The person who continues to sin is of the devil; the person who is righteous has the Spirit of God. He is born of God, and His seed remains in him.

You have a new deterrent. Once you are born again, you cannot habitually live in sin. If Jesus Christ is in you, you cannot go on carelessly, thoughtlessly, continuously, practicing a lifestyle of sin. God will discipline you because He loves you. The Holy Spirit will deter you from sin. You will be under conviction because the Holy Spirit is at work in you.

The Spirit is delivering you from the penalty of sin, the power of Satan, and the principle of self. With your new nature you have a new dynamic, a new desire, and a new deterrent.

PUT IT IN WRITING

- Are you born of God?
- Since you became a Christian, how have your desires changed?
- How do you know when the Holy Spirit is convicting you of sin?

> The Word of God and the Spirit of God in the womb of grace have made me a new person.
>
> ADRIAN ROGERS

DAY 6

LORD, MAKE US NEW

▪ PRACTICE IT

Sin is the transgression of the Law. Our rebellion proves our sinfulness. Our righteousness proclaims our sonship, and that's how we know we've been saved. Our redemption provides our salvation and redeems us from the penalty of sin, from the power of Satan, and from the principle of self. Now it's time for you to examine yourself.

> **Examine yourselves as to whether you are in the faith. Test yourselves. Do you not know yourselves, that Jesus Christ is in you?—unless indeed you are disqualified (2 Corinthians 13:5).**

Are you saved? If this were your last moment, do you absolutely know you'd go to Heaven? If you don't, it's time right now to give your heart to Jesus and to be saved. You can pray a prayer like this:

> *Dear God, I have broken Your law, and I am a sinner. My sin deserves judgment, but I need mercy. I need to be redeemed from the penalty of my sin. I need to be redeemed from the power of Satan. I need to be redeemed from the principle of self. I need to be saved from me. Jesus, thank You for paying for my sin with Your blood on the cross. Thank You for dying for me and for taking my place. Now by faith, I accept You, and I receive You into my heart as my Lord and Savior. Take control of my life right now and begin now to make me the person You want me to be. Help me never to be ashamed of You. In Jesus' Name, Amen.*

▪ PROCLAIM IT

If you prayed to receive Christ, please share your decision with another Christian you know or with your pastor. We would also like to hear about it so that we can provide you with free resources to help you grow in your new faith. Please let us know by going to **lwf.org/discover-jesus**, scrolling down the page and clicking on I BELIEVE.

Take time to examine yourself this week. You may need to have a conversation with a pastor or spiritual mentor if you have questions about your salvation. Confess and repent of any habitual sin that has crept into your life. Thank God for His unconditional forgiveness and take steps to walk in your new life. Pray for those in your circle of influence who are still bound by sin and ask for opportunities to share the Gospel with them.

> If your religion has not changed your life, you better change your religion.
>
> ADRIAN ROGERS

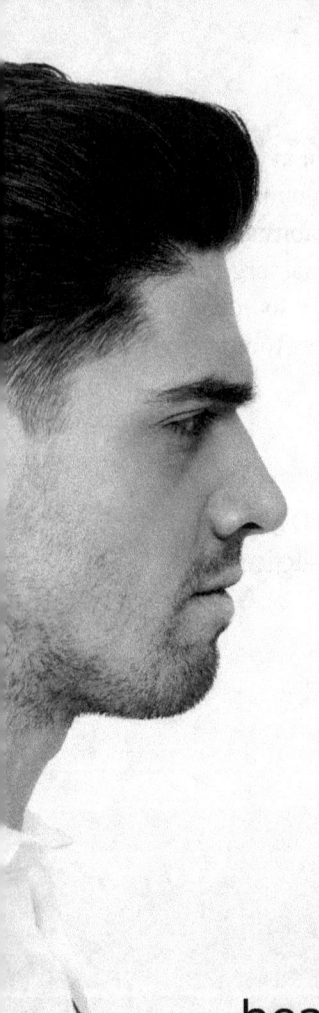
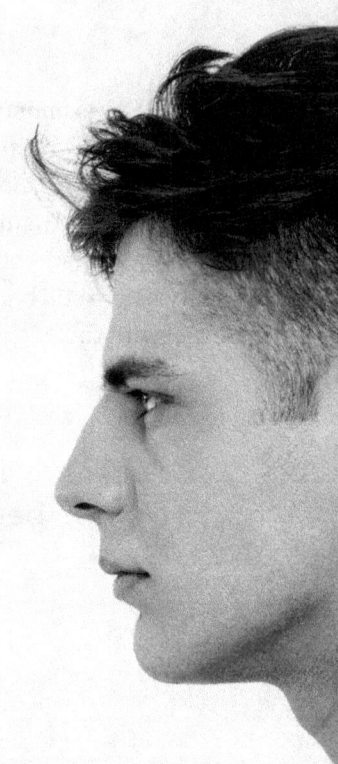

If your heart is headquarters for hate, you're on a mighty low level of life.

ADRIAN ROGERS

WEEK 9

LOVE

INTRODUCTION

Would you like to have great boldness in your faith? Would you like to be able to pray and come to God with such confidence that you absolutely know your prayer will be answered? How would you like to have sweet communion with the Lord? Would you like the Lord Jesus Christ to be in your life as a bright, burning, loving, gracious reality? As believers, we want to have assurance, confidence, and communion with the Lord every day. The key to all of that is love.

"Love" is a word we quickly overlook and take for granted. We use it to describe many things from our favorite foods to our favorite hobbies. Sometimes we use it sarcastically and imply that we love what we actually hate. This has caused the word "love" to lose its strength. But we have a legacy of love that comes from God. This kind of love causes us to operate in the world at a different level.

> **In this the children of God and the children of the devil are manifest: Whoever does not practice righteousness is not of God, nor is he who does not love his brother. For this is the message that you heard from the beginning, that we should love one another (1 John 3:10-11).**

PRAY OVER IT

Dear God, I think I know what love is, but I still struggle to love others the way that You love us. Help me to understand the blessings of love, so that I can love others. I need Your power in my life to love others this way. In Jesus' Name, Amen.

DAY 1

COUNTERFEIT LOVE

PONDER IT

To understand the higher level of love in which we are to operate, we must first identify three other lower levels in which we function

Murder—Adam had two sons. One was a martyr and one was a missionary. Cain hated Abel's religion, and Abel was a martyr for the faith.

> **For this is the message that you heard from the beginning, that we should love one another, not as Cain who was of the wicked one and murdered his brother. And why did he murder him? Because his works were evil and his brother's righteous. Do not marvel, my brethren, if the world hates you. We know that we have passed from death to life, because we love the brethren. He who does not love his brother abides in death (1 John 3:11-14).**

False religion is almost always murderous because it comes from the devil. Jesus said:

> **"...[The devil] was a murderer from the beginning..." (John 8:44b).**

> **"The thief does not come except to steal, and to kill, and to destroy" (John 10:10a).**

Satan is manipulating street gangs. Satan is whispering in the serial killer's ear. Satan is enticing well-fed, well-paid doctors to snuff out life in the womb.

Hatred—Even if you have never killed anybody, but have hate in your heart, God wrote it down in His ledger as murder.

> **Whoever hates his brother is a murderer, and you know that no murderer has eternal life abiding in him (1 John 3:15).**

Jesus said the same thing:

> "You have heard that it was said to those of old, 'You shall not murder, and whoever murders will be in danger of the judgment.' But I say to you that whoever is angry with his brother without a cause shall be in danger of the judgment" (Matthew 5:21-22a).

Indifference—Many people say, "I'm not a murderer, and I don't hate people. I just go my way and do my thing, and I let them do their thing." They're indifferent; this is not of God.

> By this we know love, because He laid down His life for us. And we also ought to lay down our lives for the brethren. But whoever has this world's goods, and sees his brother in need, and shuts up his heart from him, how does the love of God abide in him? My little children, let us not love in word or in tongue, but in deed and in truth (1 John 3:16-18).

The parable of the Good Samaritan illustrates the problem of indifference because the religious people passed the man who had been beaten and left for dead. The Samaritan was the one who showed what it truly meant to "love your neighbor as yourself."

If we are to move into an understanding of the love God has for us and the love we are to walk in, we must first understand these three lower levels of love that we are to move past.

PUT IT IN WRITING

- How are murder and hatred in your heart the same thing in God's eyes? Are you guilty of these things?
- Are there people or groups of people that you are indifferent toward? How can indifference actually harm people?

The world is full of the beater uppers and passer uppers, but thank God there are some picker uppers.

ADRIAN ROGERS

DAY 2

THE GREAT VALUE OF LOVE

▧ PONDER IT

Those who are saved are called to operate on a higher level of love—not murder, hatred, or indifference. There is immeasurable value in love.

Love is the greatest virtue. Love is greater than mountain-moving faith.

> Though I speak with the tongues of men and of angels, but have not love, I have become sounding brass or a clanging cymbal. And though I have the gift of prophecy, and understand all mysteries and all knowledge, and though I have all faith, so that I could remove mountains, but have not love, I am nothing (1 Corinthians 13:1-2).

Love is the greatest commandment. Not to love God or your brother would be the greatest sin. Jesus said:

> "'You shall love the Lord your God with all your heart, with all your soul, and with all your mind.' This is the first and great commandment. And the second is like it: 'You shall love your neighbor as yourself.' On these two commandments hang all the Law and the Prophets" (Matthew 22:37-40).

Love is the greatest testimony. Jesus Christ said:

> "By this all will know that you are My disciples, if you have love for one another" (John 13:35).

Love is the greatest motivation. The love of Jesus keeps us going.

> For the love of Christ compels us, because we judge thus: that if One died for all, then all died (2 Corinthians 5:14).

Love is the greatest investment. John gives us three blessings from learning to love like God loves. Over the next few days, we will consider these blessings.

PUT IT IN WRITING

- Why is love such an important part of the Christian life?
- Which one of these aspects of love is the most meaningful or thought-provoking to you?

> What good is it if you can
> get rid of mountains and you
> can't get rid of malice?
>
> ADRIAN ROGERS

DAY 3

A GOOD CONSCIENCE AND GREAT CONFIDENCE

PONDER IT

John gives us three blessings and benefits from learning to love the way God loves.

The blessing of a good conscience. When you have malice or hatred in your heart, you have a condemning heart. God has wired you that way. If you're saved, you cannot fail to love.

> **And by this we know that we are of the truth, and shall assure our hearts before Him. For if our heart condemns us, God is greater than our heart, and knows all things (1 John 3:19-20).**

In Bible translations, the word "conscience" and the word "heart" are often used interchangeably. When you have love in your heart, your conscience will be clear. Your conscience is not an enemy; it's your friend. It is something unique in you that God did not put into animals. A conscience is more than the part of us that feels bad when everything else feels good. It is an ability to concentrate our actions and to make moral judgments.

> **...having faith and a good conscience (1 Timothy 1:19a).**

> **This being so, I myself always strive to have a conscience without offense toward God and men (Acts 24:16).**

You can't have a good conscience without love. When you love, you'll make things right, and when you make things right, you will have transparency. If you're doubting your salvation, you'd better check up and see if there's some bitterness in your heart or some sin in your life. They are acids that will destroy your assurance. When you truly love and make things right, you will have that sweet assurance.

The blessing of great confidence. When your heart doesn't condemn you, you have confidence toward God and boldness in faith. This confidence that comes out of a clean conscience is what helps you to pray and get your prayers answered.

> **Beloved, if our heart does not condemn us, we have confidence toward God. And whatever we ask we receive from Him, because we keep His commandments and do those things that are pleasing in His sight (1 John 3:21-22).**

Having a good conscience gives you great confidence, and you can come to God, ask in His name, and see your prayers answered. Answered prayer is not for rebels or for those whose hearts are filled with hate. The Bible says:

> **If I regard iniquity in my heart, the LORD will not hear (Psalm 66:18).**

If you don't have a good conscience, you cannot have great confidence, and if you don't have great confidence, you can't get your prayers answered. It's just that plain and very practical. Love gives you a good conscience, and when love gives a good conscience, love gets a great confidence.

PUT IT IN WRITING

- How has choosing to act in love given you a clear conscience?
- When you pray, is your conscience clear and are you confident that God will answer? What do you need to do to make things right?

> You cannot pray with a condemning heart.
>
> ADRIAN ROGERS

DAY 4

A GRACIOUS COMMUNION

PONDER IT

The third blessing of love is it gives **a gracious communion.**

> **And this is His commandment: that we should believe on the name of His Son Jesus Christ and love one another, as He gave us commandment. Now he who keeps His commandments abides in Him, and He in him. And by this we know that He abides in us, by the Spirit whom He has given us (1 John 3:23-24).**

The Holy Spirit whispers to us that we belong to God. The ministry of the Holy Spirit is to take the things of Jesus and to show them to us. He makes the Lord real to us.

When you learn to love and live by love, you're going to have a good conscience. When you have a good conscience, you're going to have great confidence. When you have great confidence, you will have gracious communion.

Some Christians doubt their salvation because they don't have the witness of the Spirit. You can be saved and have absolutely no assurance because you've failed to love and you've grieved the Holy Spirit. The ministry of the Holy Spirit is to give you love, joy, peace, understanding, wisdom, power, and grace. When there is sin in your life, the voice of the Holy Spirit is gentle yet firm in His conviction. Your communion with God is broken, but He will lead you to repentance and restoration. When you abide in Christ, you will have gracious and sweet communion with God.

PUT IT IN WRITING

- What are some things that help you enjoy communion with God in your daily life?
- How do you know when the Holy Spirit is convicting you of sin?

> The progression of faith: When I accept God's acceptance of me, that's faith. Then I must accept myself; that's peace. Then I can accept you; that's love. And when you accept me, that's fellowship.
>
> ADRIAN ROGERS

DAY 5

GRIEVING THE HOLY SPIRIT

PONDER IT

Dealing with our anger, our sin, and our tongues is very important and helps us maintain communion with God and with each other. The Bible says:

> **"Be angry, and do not sin": do not let the sun go down on your wrath, nor give place to the devil. Let him who stole steal no longer, but rather let him labor, working with his hands what is good, that he may have something to give him who has need. Let no corrupt word proceed out of your mouth, but what is good for necessary edification, that it may impart grace to the hearers (Ephesians 4:26-29).**

When you have unresolved anger, you've opened the door to the devil. When you are lazy, you can't be generous. When you use your tongue to tear others down, you are not loving. The devil will ruin your life, distort your conscience, ruin your confidence, and destroy your communion. When it comes to sin, follow the leading of the Holy Spirit in you.

> **And do not grieve the Holy Spirit of God, by whom you were sealed for the day of redemption (Ephesians 4:30).**

When you give a place to the devil, you grieve the Holy Spirit because He is living in your heart when you're saved. If you have anger and sin in your heart, love is not there, but the Holy Spirit of God cannot and will not forsake you. When you were saved, you were sealed by the Holy Spirit. You are eternally secure. Paul tells us what grieves the Holy Spirit:

> **Let all bitterness, wrath, anger, clamor, and evil speaking be put away from you, with all malice (Ephesians 4:31).**

Bitterness is an unresolved hurt toward somebody who hurt you or did you wrong. It may be real or imaginary, but you perceive that somebody has wronged you. If allowed to stay in your heart, bitterness turns to wrath. The Greek word "wrath" has the idea of heat or something burning slowly. Bitterness becomes wrath, a slow burn, but then it can ignite into anger. Anger turns into clamor, or speaking loudly, and clamor turns into evil speaking. You speak hurtful things to your spouse, your children, and your parents.

Evil speaking turns into the desire to hurt somebody, which is malice. You want to hurt them financially, emotionally, or physically. You want to abuse them, and you do things in a rage. You look back and wonder how you could have done that. You let the sun go down upon your wrath and gave a place to the devil. You grieved the Holy Spirit.

The Holy Spirit is a person, and you can only grieve a person who loves you. "Grieve" is a love word. Your neighbors' kids will vex you, but your own kids will grieve you. The Holy Spirit of God loves you, but when you don't love others, you grieve the Spirit of God. He closes up and withdraws. Then you don't have sweet communion with God.

When you love, you have a good conscience. Then you have great confidence, and then you have gracious communion. Then the love of God is shed abroad in our hearts by the Holy Spirit. (See Romans 5:5.)

PUT IT IN WRITING

- What are the things that have angered you recently? What do you need to do to resolve that anger?
- Has a root of bitterness shown up in your life? How have you seen bitterness lead to other things?

> God does not change us in order to love us. He loves us in order to change us.
>
> ADRIAN ROGERS

DAY 6

GOD IS THE WAY TO LOVE

▪ PRACTICE IT

It does you no good to just grit your teeth and decide to love even if it kills you. You don't have what it takes to love like this in your own self-effort. Love is not the way to God. God is the way to love.

> **Beloved, let us love one another, for love is of God; and everyone who loves is born of God and knows God. He who does not love does not know God, for God is love (1 John 4:7-8).**

The only way that you can love is to have the love of God in your heart. Are you born of God? Have you come to the Lord in absolute sincerity and trusted Him to forgive your sins?

> **Whoever believes that Jesus is the Christ is born of God, and everyone who loves Him who begot also loves him who is begotten of Him (1 John 5:1).**

Love is not an emotional matter. It may show in emotions, but your emotions are the shallowest part of your nature. Salvation is the deepest work of God. He doesn't do the deepest work in the shallowest part. God is listening, and from the moment you turn to Him, a river of love begins to flow in you. Love is of God. You'll never be able to love your wife, your children, or your neighbors as you ought until you give your heart to Jesus. Love is not the way to God; God is the way to love, and Jesus is the way to the Father. The legacy of love is a good conscience, great confidence, and gracious communion.

If you've never received Jesus Christ as your personal Savior and Lord, you can do so right now. Pray a prayer like this if you're not certain that you're saved.

> *Dear God, I know You love me, and I know You want to save me. Thank You, Jesus, for paying for my sin with Your blood on the cross. By faith, I receive You as my Lord and Savior. Forgive*

my sin and save me. Thank You for saving me. I receive it by faith, I will make it public, and I will not be ashamed of You. I will follow You the rest of my life wherever You lead me, not in order to be saved, but because I have been saved and because I love You. In Jesus' Name, Amen.

PROCLAIM IT

If you prayed to receive Christ, please share your decision with another Christian you know or with your pastor. We would also like to hear about it so that we can provide you with free resources to help you grow in your new faith. Please let us know by going to **lwf.org/discover-jesus,** scrolling down the page and clicking on I BELIEVE.

Spend time with God asking Him to show you your sin and to show you how to love those around you. Then act in faith based on what the Holy Spirit asks you to do. Go and love others in the strength of the Lord and the power of the Holy Spirit.

Love is not the way to God.
God is the way to love.

ADRIAN ROGERS

The devil would rather get you to believe a wrong thing than to do a wrong thing because the thought is the father of the deed.

ADRIAN ROGERS

WEEK 10

ANTICHRISTS

INTRODUCTION

Christians are called believers, but unbelief can be a virtue as well. John tells us what we are to believe and what we are not to believe.

> **Beloved, do not believe every spirit, but test the spirits, whether they are of God; because many false prophets have gone out into the world (1 John 4:1).**

Somehow, we get the idea that we're supposed to believe anything and everything because we are believers. Faith is no better than its origin and no better than its object. Faith is not just simply deciding what you want to believe and then believing it. Faith is not trying to make yourself believe what you feel is not true. Biblical faith is getting a word from God and acting on that.

> **But without faith it is impossible to please Him, for he who comes to God must believe that He is, and that He is a rewarder of those who diligently seek Him (Hebrews 11:6).**

Without faith it's impossible to please God, so it's extremely dangerous to live without faith. But even more dangerous is belief in the wrong thing. This week we will look at the Christ we are to believe and the Antichrist whom we must not believe.

PRAY OVER IT

Dear God, These days, we're looked upon as unkind if we don't put our arms around everybody and say that their faith is just as good as ours. But You've sent Your Son into this world to be the Savior of the world. On that rock, I stand. Give me discernment as I walk through this world and lead others in Your truth. In Jesus' Name, Amen.

DAY 1

WHEN UNBELIEF IS A VIRTUE

PONDER IT

In the middle of a passage on love, John warns us about false prophets. Sometimes we think that to be loving, we must be soft-headed. But being loving doesn't mean we have to put our arms around everyone and embrace their faith. Not everything spiritual is of God.

Beloved, do not believe every spirit, but test the spirits, whether they are of God; because many false prophets have gone out into the world (1 John 4:1).

If the devil can get you to believe a wrong thing, that belief will lead you to do a wrong thing. The devil strategically sets up a false belief system.

For as he thinks in his heart, so is he (Proverbs 23:7a).

Just as the Bible teaches us what to believe, the Bible very clearly teaches us what not to believe. We are encouraged to test the spirits to see whether they are of God. God tells us to test our faith.

Test all things; hold fast what is good (1 Thessalonians 5:21).

What reasons do we have for believing what we believe? What is the difference between Christ and Antichrist? Behind every prophet, there's a spirit: the spirit of Satan or the Spirit of the Almighty. We're bombarded by all kinds of teachings and philosophies, and we must be able to discern what is true.

PUT IT IN WRITING

- What is the difference between being soft-hearted and soft-headed? How should we interact with people who believe something different from us?
- How do you know whether something is true? What are some of the tests you use to discern truth?

> The faith that can't be tested can't be trusted.
>
> ADRIAN ROGERS

DAY 2

TEST THE SPIRITS

PONDER IT

The Bible gives us some specific ways to test prophets to determine whether they are of God.

Test them by their methods. Their methods are often subtle or hidden. The Bible said the serpent in the garden was more cunning and crafty than any beast of the field. The devil is the father of lies, and he knows that the best lies sound the most like the truth.

> **For certain men have crept in unnoticed, who long ago were marked out for this condemnation, ungodly men, who turn the grace of our God into lewdness and deny the only Lord God and our Lord Jesus Christ (Jude 4).**

False prophets can creep into the church without raising any red flags. Unbelief and false doctrine secretly creep in through the side door. His method is not so much a denial as it is a misrepresentation.

Test them by their morals. When the Bible says, "they turned the grace of God into lewdness," it means "immorality." They try to convince people that if they are saved by grace, they can live any way they want. They've turned the grace of God into lewdness.

Test them by their motives. False prophets are covetous. With slick talk, they exploit people and take advantage of them financially, politically, or personally. Even if they may not seem to care for money or political power, they want to be seen as important.

> **And many will follow their destructive ways, because of whom the way of truth will be blasphemed. By covetousness they will exploit you with deceptive words (2 Peter 2:2-3a).**

Test them by their ministry. If you want to test a prophet, look at the fruit of his or her ministry. Measure prophets by those who are following them. Jesus said you'll know them by their fruits.

"Beware of false prophets, who come to you in sheep's clothing, but inwardly they are ravenous wolves. You will know them by their fruits. Do men gather grapes from thornbushes or figs from thistles?" (Matthew 7:15-16).

Test them by their message. If their message does not involve Jesus Christ, you should beware.

By this you know the Spirit of God: Every spirit that confesses that Jesus Christ has come in the flesh is of God, and every spirit that does not confess that Jesus Christ has come in the flesh is not of God. And this is the spirit of the Antichrist, which you have heard was coming, and is now already in the world (1 John 4:2-3).

In the word "antichrist," the prefix anti- means "against" and it can also mean "instead of." Satan is against Christ, so he brings in a substitute instead of Christ. A false prophet will probably claim to believe in Jesus.

Don't let somebody lead you to another spirit. Don't let somebody teach you about another gospel. As Paul told us, Satan is able to transform himself to appear as an angel of light. (See 2 Corinthians 11:14.)

PUT IT IN WRITING

- What are the false prophets or false teachings you see people in your community believing?
- When you consider their methods, motives, morals, ministry, and message, what do you discover?

When we stand upon the Word of God, Satan's kingdom begins to tremble.

ADRIAN ROGERS

DAY 3

TEST BY THE WORD OF GOD

▪ PONDER IT

To test anything, you must have a standard or a measuring rod. You must have set criteria to accurately test someone or something. We can use the Word of God, the Son of God, and the Spirit of God as our standards. **Test the spirits by the Word of God.**

> **You are of God, little children, and have overcome them, because He who is in you is greater than he who is in the world. They are of the world. Therefore they speak as of the world, and the world hears them. We are of God. He who knows God hears us; he who is not of God does not hear us. By this we know the spirit of truth and the spirit of error (1 John 4:4-6).**

John was an apostle, and with the other apostles, they brought the Word of God. They were firsthand witnesses to the life, death, and resurrection of Jesus.

> **That which was from the beginning, which we have heard, which we have seen with our eyes, which we have looked upon, and our hands have handled, concerning the Word of life—the life was manifested, and we have seen, and bear witness, and declare to you that eternal life which was with the Father and was manifested to us—that which we have seen and heard we declare to you (1 John 1:1-3a).**

The apostles were those who saw Jesus, who heard Jesus, who were anointed and appointed to bring the Word of God. The Church is built on the foundation of their testimony.

> **...having been built on the foundation of the apostles and prophets, Jesus Christ Himself being the chief cornerstone (Ephesians 2:20)**

The Church is built upon the foundation of the apostles and the prophets who brought us the Word of God. So, when new "prophets" come along, you check them out by the Word of God, not some sort of a feeling you get.

The question we need to ask is: What does the Word of God say? The devil came to Jesus in the wilderness to tempt Him. Jesus dealt with the devil by using the Word of God. Three times Jesus said, "It is written…" Jesus used the sword of the Word of God to resist Satan's temptations. There is incredible power in the Word of God.

I will worship toward Your holy temple, and praise Your name for Your lovingkindness and Your truth; for You have magnified Your word above all Your name (Psalm 138:2).

If you don't know the Word of God and how to rightly handle it, you're going to be an easy target for false prophets. You won't know how to test the spirits. When you test the spirits by the Word of God, everything else will follow.

PUT IT IN WRITING

- How well do you know the Word of God? How have you used it to resist temptation or to test false prophets?
- In your current season of life, what does it look like to study God's Word? What are the routines or habits that help you stay in God's Word?

> When some false prophet comes, if you use the Word of God, it will go through that business like a white-hot cannonball through a crate of eggs.
>
> ADRIAN ROGERS

DAY 4

TEST BY THE SON OF GOD

PONDER IT

Not only do you test a false prophet by the Word of God, but you also **test a false prophet by the Son of God.**

> **By this you know the Spirit of God: Every spirit that confesses that Jesus Christ has come in the flesh is of God, and every spirit that does not confess that Jesus Christ has come in the flesh is not of God. And this is the spirit of the Antichrist, which you have heard was coming, and is now already in the world (1 John 4:2-3).**

John uses two names: Jesus, which is His human name, and Christ, which is His divine title. Christ is not His last name; it is His title. Christ means Messiah, the Anointed One, the Appointed One. Jesus Christ is man and Messiah at the same time. There is no one else like Jesus Christ.

This is the fundamental doctrine of our faith: that God stepped out of Heaven and took on human flesh. We call that the incarnation, which means "in the flesh." When Jesus Christ took on humanity, He did not lay it aside when He went back to Heaven. He took it with Him. For all eternity, He will have a body of flesh.

When the Apostle John was an aged man on the island of Patmos, he had a vision of Christ and described Him as One like the Son of Man. (See Revelation 1:12-13.) Jesus became the Son of Man so that you might become sons and daughters of God. Jesus was born of a virgin, so that you might be born again. For all eternity, you have a high priest who understands the feeling of your infirmities. When you get to Heaven, you will see Jesus and the nail scars in His hands that He will bear for all eternity.

This is not easy to understand or grasp. Jesus is as much man as if He were not God at all, but He is as much God as if He were not man at all. He's not half God and half man, not all man and no God, not all

God and no man. He is the God-Man, and there will never be another like Him.

Anyone who doesn't believe that Jesus is God is of the spirit of antichrist. Don't let somebody come along and claim to believe in Jesus as a man, the great prophet, the great teacher, and deny His deity. It is a heresy to deny His humanity or His deity.

> **Who is a liar but he who denies that Jesus is the Christ? He is antichrist who denies the Father and the Son (1 John 2:22).**

> **For many deceivers have gone out into the world who do not confess Jesus Christ as coming in the flesh. This is a deceiver and an antichrist...Whoever transgresses and does not abide in the doctrine of Christ does not have God. He who abides in the doctrine of Christ has both the Father and the Son. If anyone comes to you and does not bring this doctrine, do not receive him into your house nor greet him (2 John 1:7, 9-10).**

PUT IT IN WRITING

- What do other religions believe about Jesus? What do you believe about Jesus?
- Why is the incarnation of Jesus so important for the Christian faith? What are the consequences of removing this piece?

> There is no way you can be right with God and be wrong about Jesus.
>
> ADRIAN ROGERS

DAY 5

TEST BY THE SPIRIT OF GOD

PONDER IT

The last test is to **test false prophets by the Spirit of God.**

> **By this we know the spirit of truth and the spirit of error (1 John 4:6b).**

A cord of three strands is not easily broken, and we have the Word of God, the Son of God, and the Spirit of God. You will struggle to understand the Bible unless the Holy Spirit teaches you. The Bible says Satan is so clever that he would deceive the very elect if it were possible. (See Matthew 24:24.) You must have the Spirit of God to help you understand the Word of God to know the Son of God.

> **"And when he brings out his own sheep, he goes before them; and the sheep follow him, for they know his voice" (John 10:4)**

The Holy Spirit of God takes the things of God and makes them real to you.

> **John answered and said, "A man can receive nothing unless it has been given to him from heaven" (John 3:27).**

> **Therefore I make known to you that no one speaking by the Spirit of God calls Jesus accursed, and no one can say that Jesus is Lord except by the Holy Spirit (1 Corinthians 12:3).**

The only way you were able to make Jesus the Lord of your life was by the Holy Spirit. The Holy Spirit of God takes the things of Jesus and shows them to us to make them real to us.

■ PUT IT IN WRITING

- How do you recognize the voice of the Holy Spirit in your life?
- In what ways has the Spirit of God helped you understand the Word of God and know the Son of God?

> We have the object of our faith, the Lord Jesus. We have the record of our faith, the Word of God. And we have the energizer of our faith, the Holy Spirit of God.
>
> ADRIAN ROGERS

DAY 6

YOUR CHOICE

▦ PRACTICE IT

A radio has two bands: AM and FM. You can tune into the signals that come from the AM or FM. Both are constantly sending out signals, but you get to choose which channel you listen to.

Today there are two signals coming out in the world: the antichrist message and the Father's message. Both are being broadcast all the time. But you can choose which message you listen to. You can turn the dial of your attention in either direction.

Two things that are different can't both be right. They could both be wrong, but if they are different, they both can't be right. The world we're living in today wants to say that both can be true at the same time.

In postmodernism, everybody creates their own reality, and everybody decides for themselves what is true. But there is a right and a wrong. The Spirit of Christ and the spirit of antichrist are both at work in the world today. As Christians, we must believe the Bible is the Word of God and Jesus is the Son of God. The Holy Spirit of God will help you understand that.

If you have not decided to trust Jesus as your Savior and make Him Lord of your life, the Holy Spirit may be prompting you to make that decision today. You can trust what the Word of God says about the Son of God. The Spirit of God will give you the words to pray and invite Jesus into your life.

▦ PROCLAIM IT

If you want to know more about how to become a Christian, you can talk with another Christian you know or with your pastor. We can provide you with free resources to help you grow in your faith. Please let us know by going to **lwf.org/discover-jesus**, scrolling down the page and clicking on I BELIEVE.

If you are concerned that you have been following a false prophet or believing false teaching based on the tests from this week, pray and ask God about what your next step of faith is. Pray for those in your community who don't believe Jesus is the Son of Man and the Son of God. Ask God to give you an opportunity to share the truth of the Gospel with them.

> It will be a great day in America when Americans turn from religion to faith in the Lord Jesus Christ.
>
> ADRIAN ROGERS

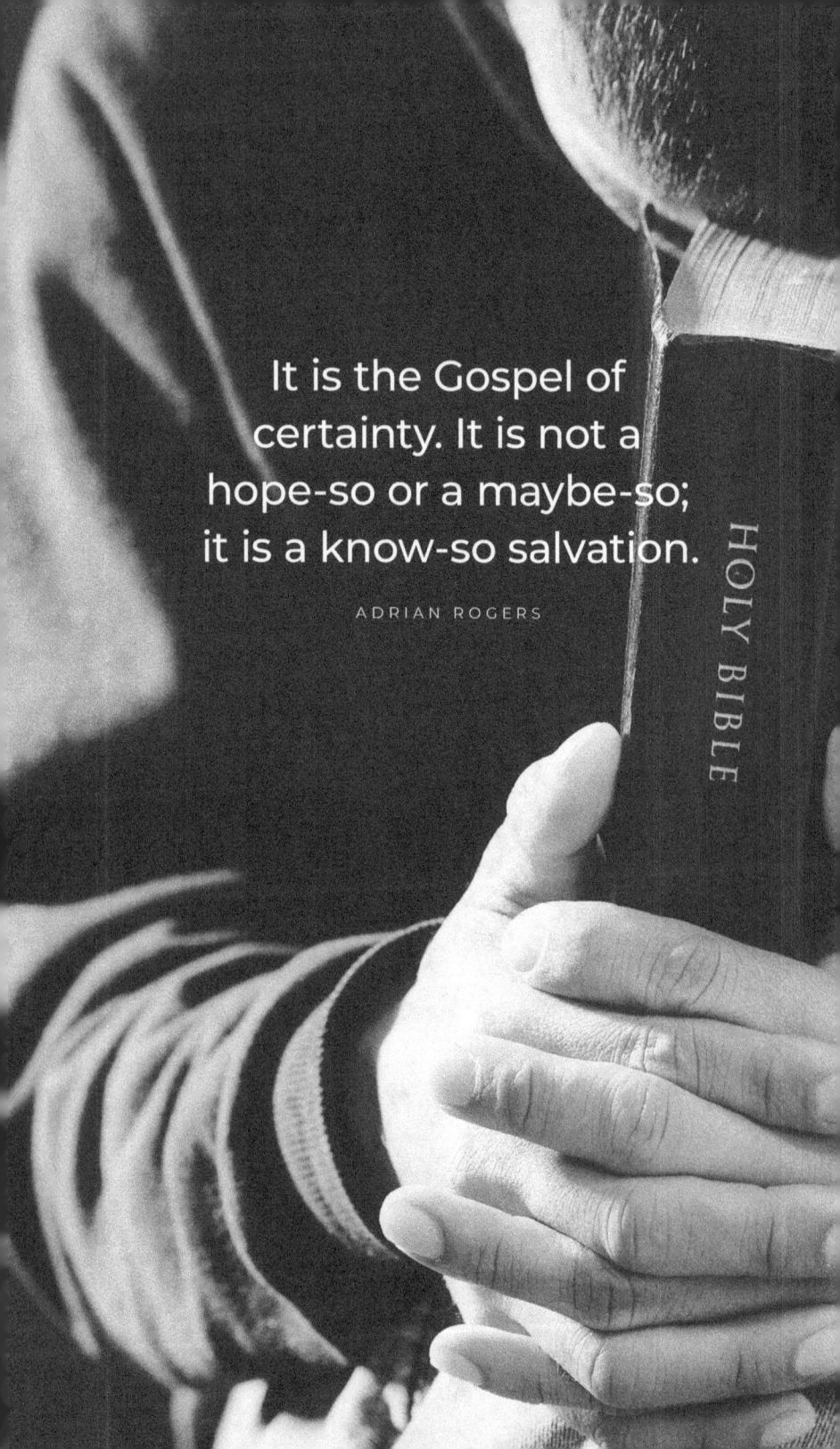

WEEK 11

ASSURANCE

INTRODUCTION

One of the great promises in all of Scripture is that we can know that we know that we know that we're saved—Heaven-born and Heaven-bound. If you are not saved, you need to be saved so you can know it. If you are saved, you ought to know it. You can know, beyond the shadow of any doubt, that you are saved. There are only two categories before God: the saved and the lost, the saints and the ain'ts. You are in one category or another, and you can't be in both.

While it's true that only God can say who is saved, we can find out what God says in the Bible. When we find out what God says, then we can say what God says and be sure.

> **Whoever believes that Jesus is the Christ is born of God, and everyone who loves Him who begot also loves him who is begotten of Him. By this we know that we love the children of God, when we love God and keep His commandments. For this is the love of God, that we keep His commandments. And His commandments are not burdensome. For whatever is born of God overcomes the world. And this is the victory that has overcome the world—our faith. Who is he who overcomes the world, but he who believes that Jesus is the Son of God? (1 John 5:1-5).**

PRAY OVER IT

Dear God, I confess that sometimes I worry I might not really be saved. I wonder what will happen when I die, and if everything I believe is true. Comfort my heart this week with the truth of Your Word. Help me to know the truth of my salvation so I can share it with others. In Jesus' Name, Amen.

DAY 1

THE ATONING WORK

▪ PONDER IT

The Gospel of John was written to tell us how to be saved, and 1 John was written to tell us how to know we're saved. More than 40 times in five chapters, John uses the word "know." Another key word is a Greek word that is translated in different ways as "witness, record, testimony, and testify." God gave us a witness so that we could know.

First, there is the **certainty that comes from the atoning work of Christ.** It speaks of what Jesus Christ did to redeem us, and it said that He came by water and blood.

> **This is He who came by water and blood—Jesus Christ; not only by water, but by water and blood (1 John 5:6a).**

When Jesus Christ was dying, the Roman soldiers wanted to make certain that those who had been crucified were dead. The Jews wanted them dead before the sun set and the Sabbath began. The soldiers were breaking the legs of those who'd been crucified in order to hasten death. But when they came to Jesus, He was already dead.

> **But when they came to Jesus and saw that He was already dead, they did not break His legs. But one of the soldiers pierced His side with a spear, and immediately blood and water came out (John 19:33-34).**

Blood and water poured out of the wounded side of Jesus. The pericardial pleural fluid that encases the heart is a watery substance. But sometimes in great duress, medical experts tell us that plasma separates. There was fluid around the heart, which reflected the physical agony that Jesus endured.

But what is the message of blood and water? It is the blood that cleanses from sin and removes the penalty of sin. (See Romans 6:23 and Hebrews 9:22.) Jesus took your sin to that cross, and with His blood, He paid sin's penalty. The water speaks of that which continues to cleanse. Together, the water and blood speak not only of salvation, but also of sanctification.

> **And the Word became flesh and dwelt among us, and we beheld His glory, the glory as of the only begotten of the Father, full of grace and truth (John 1:14).**

The "Word" is Jesus. The "logos" was made flesh and dwelt among us. The word "dwelt" is the word for "tabernacled." Jesus "tabernacled" among us. That tabernacle in the Old Testament was a place of worship for the Israelites as they journeyed in the wilderness and also a prophecy of Jesus. The tabernacle had a brazen altar where the blood of animal sacrifices was shed. Past that altar was a great basin called a "laver." The blood is shed at the altar, and the water cleanses at the laver. The priests went through the blood and the water to get to the holy of holies. The blood deals with the penalty of sin; the water deals with the pollution of sin. Jesus tabernacled among us and came by blood and water. It's significant that when they put that spear in His side, blood and water came out. There is certainty from the atoning work of Christ.

PUT IT IN WRITING

- Why are both blood (atoning) and water (cleansing) important for our salvation?
- What does the continuity of the symbol of blood and water from the Old Testament to the New Testament tell you about the character of God?

> Jesus literally died of a broken heart. There was no agony like the agony of Jesus.
>
> ADRIAN ROGERS

DAY 2

THE WITNESS OF THE SPIRIT TO YOU

PONDER IT

Secondly, there is **certainty from the abiding witness of the Spirit.** The Holy Spirit takes the water and the blood and bears witness to your faith.

> **And it is the Spirit who bears witness, because the Spirit is truth. For there are three that bear witness in heaven: the Father, the Word, and the Holy Spirit; and these three are one. And there are three that bear witness on earth: the Spirit, the water, and the blood; and these three agree as one. If we receive the witness of men, the witness of God is greater; for this is the witness of God which He has testified of His Son (1 John 5:6b-9).**

The word "if" can also be translated "since." You have the atoning work, but the Holy Spirit takes the atoning work, and He testifies of it. He gives an abiding witness to you on the inside.

You already believe men and receive their witness as truth. Before you go out to a new restaurant, you read reviews and ask people for recommendations. When you fly on a plane, even though you have never seen or met the pilots or examined the airplane, you trust that the pilots know how to fly, and that people have decided the plane is worthy of flight. When the doctor writes a prescription, you trust that the doctor and the pharmacist know how to do their jobs, even though you can't read all the ingredients in the medicine. We receive the witness of men every day. That requires some level of faith.

But even more than the witness of men, the Holy Spirit witnesses **to** us. Before we're even saved, the Holy Spirit is telling us about Jesus and bearing witness to the truth. Jesus said this about the ministry of the Holy Spirit:

> "However, when He, the Spirit of truth, has come, He will guide you into all truth; for He will not speak on His own authority, but whatever He hears He will speak; and He will tell you things to come. He will glorify Me, for He will take of what is Mine and declare it to you" (John 16:13-14).

You live by faith every day of your life, and you put your faith in two-legged men who are fallible and sometimes lie. But the Holy Spirit is truth; He cannot lie. If you want to believe, the Holy Spirit will enable you to believe. Jesus said:

> "And the Father Himself, who sent Me, has testified of Me. You have neither heard His voice at any time, nor seen His form. But you do not have His word abiding in you, because whom He sent, Him you do not believe. You search the Scriptures, for in them you think you have eternal life; and these are they which testify of Me. But you are not willing to come to Me that you may have life" (John 5:37-40).

When the Word of God is preached, the Holy Spirit of God witnesses to you and confirms the truth.

PUT IT IN WRITING

- Do you have the Holy Spirit residing in you? How do you know?
- When you look back at when you first believed, how do you see the Holy Spirit at work? How did you know the Gospel was true?

> Asking God to explain Himself would be like asking Einstein to explain the theory of relativity to your dog.
>
> ADRIAN ROGERS

DAY 3

THE WITNESS OF THE SPIRIT *IN* YOU AND *THROUGH* YOU

PONDER IT

Not only does the Holy Spirit witness **to** you, but He also witnesses **in** you. When you receive Christ, the Holy Spirit comes into you.

> **He who believes in the Son of God has the witness *in* himself (1 John 5:10a, emphasis added).**

Suppose Bob, Jim, and Roger are arguing about apple pie. Jim says, "I don't believe there is such a thing as apple pie. It doesn't even exist." Bob says, "I believe it exists, but it's no good and not worth eating." Roger has already eaten two pieces and is getting ready to ingest a third. Are the opinions of Bob and Jim going to keep Roger from eating the apple pie that he knows is good? Of course not! He has the witness inside of him that apple pie exists and is very good. That is the reason a Christian with an experience is never at the mercy of an infidel with an argument. One way to find out whether apple pie is good or not is to taste and see. The Bible says:

> **Oh, taste and see that the Lord is good; blessed is the man who trusts in Him! (Psalm 34:8).**

The witness of the Holy Spirit is not an emotional feeling, goosebumps, or liver shivers. If you base your assurance of your salvation on what you feel, your assurance will go up and down with the condition of your liver. If you live by emotions, you will constantly be on a roller coaster. The witness of the Spirit is far deeper than emotions.

However, the assurance of your salvation can show up in your emotions. When it dawns on you that you know you're saved, you may get very excited about it. Emotions are good and natural, but that is not the witness of the Spirit. When God's Spirit speaks to you that you belong to Him, you can definitely get emotional.

Many times, we try to make everybody else have the same emotional experience we have. We don't have to impose an emotional experience on someone for them to be saved. The witness of the Spirit does not require an emotional experience.

After the Holy Spirit of God witnesses **to** you and **in** you, then the Holy Spirit can witness **through** you.

> **"But you shall receive power when the Holy Spirit has come upon you; and you shall be witnesses to Me in Jerusalem, and in all Judea and Samaria, and to the end of the earth" (Acts 1:8).**

When you have the assurance of your salvation, it's much easier to be a witness.

> **And we are His witnesses to these things, and so also is the Holy Spirit whom God has given to those who obey Him (Acts 5:32).**

When you share the Gospel, whether the message is received does not depend upon eloquence or logic. It depends on the Holy Spirit of God and the work He is doing.

PUT IT IN WRITING

- How has the Holy Spirit confirmed in you that you belong to God? What spiritual practices have helped you discern the voice of the Spirit in your life?
- When have you felt the Holy Spirit speaking through you to others? Who are the people with whom God is prompting you to share the Gospel?

> You don't explain the witness of the Spirit; you receive it.
>
> ADRIAN ROGERS

DAY 4

THE WORD OF THE FATHER

PONDER IT

These three things work together to confirm the truth of salvation: the atoning work of the Savior, the abiding witness of the Spirit, and **the Word of the Father.** God's Word is the source of our certainty, the basis of our belief, and the way you can know you are saved.

> **...he who does not believe God has made Him a liar, because he has not believed the testimony that God has given of His Son...These things I have written to you who believe in the name of the Son of God, that you may know that you have eternal life (1 John 5:10b, 13a).**

God gave us a record: the Bible. It has one central message from Genesis to Revelation: Jesus saves. This book was not written to tell you what happens in Heaven; it was written to tell you how to go to Heaven.

If you don't believe the Bible, you're calling God a liar. If someone tells you the way to get somewhere, and you respond that you are trying to believe what he is saying, then you are saying he must be a liar part of the time. If you don't follow the directions, you don't think the person who gave them to you is trustworthy. God's no liar.

Because of the atoning work of Christ, the abiding witness of the Spirit, and the affirming Word of God, you can know you have eternal life.

■ **PUT IT IN WRITING**
- Why is it important to believe that what the Bible says is true?
- How have the atoning work of Christ, the abiding witness of the Spirit, and the affirming Word of God worked together to help you know whether you are saved?

> We do not live by explanations;
> we live by promises.
>
> ADRIAN ROGERS

DAY 5

SOURCE, SUBSTANCE AND SURETY

PONDER IT

Jesus Christ is the source of life. You don't have life if you don't have Him. Apart from Jesus, there is no eternal life.

> **And this is the testimony: that God has given us eternal life, and this life is in His Son (1 John 5:11).**

Jesus is the substance of life. Jesus Christ is to your spirit what blood is to your body. It is not a religion about Him or simply following His precepts. It is Christ in you, the hope of glory.

> **He who has the Son has life; he who does not have the Son of God does not have life (1 John 5:12).**

Other teachers may point to life, but Jesus claimed to be the way, the truth, and the life. (See John 14:6.)

Jesus is the surety of life. Because of Jesus, you can know beyond a shadow of a doubt that you will go to Heaven.

> **These things I have written to you who believe in the name of the Son of God, that you may know that you have eternal life, and that you may continue to believe in the name of the Son of God (1 John 5:13).**

There is a three-fold cord that officially confirms your relationship to Christ: the atoning work of Christ, the abiding witness of the Spirit, the affirming Word of the Father.

PUT IT IN WRITING

- How would you prove to someone else that you are saved?
- What is keeping you from believing that you are truly saved?

> Christianity is Christ. It's not a creed, a code, or a cause; it is Christ.
>
> ADRIAN ROGERS

DAY 6

BELIEVE AND BE SAVED

◼ PRACTICE IT

A little boy was in a revival meeting, and the pastor preached from the Gospel of John:

> **"Most assuredly, I say to you, he who hears My word and believes in Him who sent Me has everlasting life, and shall not come into judgment, but has passed from death into life" (John 5:24).**

The boy believed it and was saved, but the devil always counter attacks. On the way home, the little fellow said the devil began to whisper to him, saying, "You're not saved. You don't feel just right. You don't deserve it. You're not good enough." All the way home, the devil was just following that little boy.

The boy sat on the couch, trying to get it all sorted out because he wanted absolute assurance that he was saved. He remembered the verse the preacher used. The boy said, "I have everlasting life. I've done it. The Word says so."

He imagined that Satan was lurking under the couch. He took the Bible and stuck it under the couch and said, "Devil, read it for yourself." From there on, his doubt left.

When the devil gets on your trail, don't argue with him. He's not worth it. Point him to the Word of God and step out of the argument. Let him argue with God Himself. The Bible says clearly and plainly:

> **He who has the Son has life; he who does not have the Son of God does not have life (1 John 5:12).**

Do you have Him? The Holy Spirit of God is telling you there was One who came by water and blood, who died for you. Even now the Holy Spirit is telling you that what you are reading is right and true.

He is witnessing to you right now. You receive Him now by praying a prayer like this:

> *Dear God, I know You love me, and I know You want to save me. Jesus, thank You for paying for my sin with Your blood on the cross. I believe You're the Son of God. I believe You rose from the dead, and I now receive You as my Lord and Savior forever. Save me and help me never to be ashamed of You. Save me by Your grace and keep me for Your glory. I will make it public. I will not be ashamed of You. I will live for You the rest of my life as You give me strength. In Jesus' Name, Amen.*

▪ PROCLAIM IT

If you prayed to receive Christ, please share your decision with another Christian you know or with your pastor. We would also like to hear about it so that we can provide you with free resources to help you grow in your new faith. Please let us know by going to **lwf.org/discover-jesus,** scrolling down the page and clicking on I BELIEVE.

If you still have questions about whether you are saved, spend some time speaking with a Christian mentor or a pastor. Share what you have been learning this week and the questions you have. If you know you are saved, pray for those you know who are not saved. Ask God to give you opportunities to share the good news of the Gospel with them.

> When the devil gets on your trail, don't argue with him. He's not worth it. Point him to the Word of God and step out of the argument.
>
> ADRIAN ROGERS

LISTEN NOW

Use this QR Code to listen to the original messages from Pastor Adrian Rogers' series, "The Sweetest Fellowship This Side of Heaven." Each message in the list corresponds to a chapter in this Bible Study.

lwf.org/audio-cda160

The Sweetest Fellowship This Side of Heaven

Things That Hinder Fellowship

Birthmarks of the Believer

How to be a Growing Christian

Your Friendly Enemy

Living in the Last Days

When We All Get to Heaven

Real Salvation

The Legacy of Love

Will Christmas Be Christ or Anti-Christ?

How to Be Absolutely Sure

DISCUSSION GUIDE

LIFE IS SWEETER WITH JESUS

This study is based on a series of messages Pastor Rogers preached on various passages from John's epistles. The content focuses mainly on 1 John but pulls in passages from 2 John and 3 John as well. John's purpose in this text was to confirm that what the saints of the Early Church believed was true.

KEY QUESTIONS ADDRESSED IN THIS STUDY

- What does it mean to be saved?
- What do I do with sin in my life?
- How do I identify false teachings and the tactics of our enemy?
- What can I expect in the Last Days and how should I live?
- How can I know I am truly saved?

KEY CONCEPTS

- Salvation comes through faith in Jesus Christ.
- We can confess our sin and experience God's forgiveness.
- The Holy Spirit works in our lives after we are saved to sanctify us.
- We ought to love others because God loved us.
- Life is sweeter when we believe what God's Word says and act in faith.

PREPARING TO LEAD/FACILITATE EACH SESSION

Read through the weekly lesson in the Bible Study and spend time writing your answers to the questions. Encourage the group participants to do the same. Before the session, review the **Discussion Questions** and the **Prayer & Action Point**. The questions are meant to build and increase in depth. If you have time, listen to the Adrian Rogers message for each week. He includes additional information and interesting stories that may not be included in the text of the Bible Study. When appropriate, you may want to invite your group to listen to specific sections of Pastor Rogers' messages.

CONDUCTING EACH SESSION

At the beginning of each session, read the **Introduction** from the Bible Study book to your group, then open discussion by asking participants to share their biggest questions or takeaways from the week. Please keep in mind that you do not have to have the answers to the questions people ask. Sometimes the act of asking the question is helpful, and having a safe place to be curious about our faith is important. Allow the group to answer the question or commit to finding the answers together before the next session. If someone asks questions that are too far off the topic of the study, you may want to meet with that person outside the session or get the support of a pastor or church leader.

Next, pray and ask God to guide your conversation, and then lead your group through the **Discussion Questions.** Your role is to facilitate the lessons and the conversation. Make sure everyone has opportunity to share. Avoid the temptation to fill silence with talking or lecturing. The silence can allow time for everyone to process, think, and listen to the Holy Spirit. You can also invite participants to go deeper by asking questions such as "Why?" or "Why not?" or saying, "Tell me more." You can ask participants to clarify answers by saying "Can you help me understand...?"

The questions are intentionally ordered so that the first two questions are typically questions everyone can answer. They are meant to get people talking. If you want to keep them talking, avoid fixing and judging. Do not try to fix their problems or tell them what they are doing wrong. If others in the group try to do this, find a polite way to bring the focus back to sharing personal experiences.

The questions will increase in depth. You can jump around based on which questions feel the most applicable to your group. Be listening to the Holy Spirit as well to see if other questions come to mind. As the facilitator, you are listening to the group and the Holy Spirit at the same time. Your situation each week can change based on participant feedback and questions. You are leading your group as God is leading you. Stay focused on the content and the context of the study, but also be attentive to where the Spirit is moving.

The last question asks group members to apply what they have learned to their lives. You may invite participants to silently reflect or write down their answers until they are more comfortable in the group. If people share their answers aloud, avoid judgment statements that are positive or negative. This will help people avoid comparison and people pleasing. Simply say, "Thank you for sharing" or "We will be praying for that with you."

Encourage participants to find one or two other people with whom to discuss the **Prayer & Action Point.** It is meant to challenge them to apply the main teaching in the lesson in a practical way and open the door for accountability. Participants can share their answers to the question and then pray for each other. Remember to affirm the importance of confidentiality within the group as participants share.

WEEK 1

FELLOWSHIP

LISTEN TO THE SERMON

lwf.org/audio-2099

DISCUSSION QUESTIONS

1. What was your biggest takeaway from this week's study? What questions do you have after going through the study?
2. What would be the key elements of living your best life? What would you have or do if you were living your ideal life?
3. What do you know about what other religions believe about Jesus? How is that different from what Christians believe about Jesus?
4. In what ways was Jesus like us? In what ways was He not like us?
5. How have you explained what you believe about Jesus to other people? Who taught you about Jesus?
6. What does it mean to you that you are a "partaker of the divine nature" if you are a believer? How should this fact affect how you live your life?
7. Where have you been looking for joy? What would it look like for you to find joy in the Lord?

PRAYER & ACTION POINT

As a group, spend time thanking God for the fellowship you can have with Him through Christ. Pray for those in your community who do not know Jesus and ask God for opportunities to share the Gospel with them.

WEEK 2

SIN

LISTEN TO THE SERMON
lwf.org/audio-2101

DISCUSSION QUESTIONS

1. What was your biggest takeaway from this week's study? What questions do you have after going through the study?
2. When you make a mistake, what is your first reaction? What do you naturally tend to do?
3. What are some ways our culture or other religions deal with the problem of sin? What is the difference between living in the dark and living in the light?
4. The two vital relationships we have as believers are sonship and fellowship. Which one do you struggle to live out?
5. How are deception and lying related to sin?
6. How is the conviction of the Holy Spirit different from the accusation of Satan? How do you know the difference?
7. Are you confident your sin has been forgiven? What keeps you from believing God has forgiven you?

PRAYER & ACTION POINT

With a partner, spend time confessing your sin silently or aloud. Then remind each other of the truth of God's Word found in 1 John 1:9.

WEEK 3

NEW BIRTH

LISTEN TO THE SERMON
lwf.org/audio-2103

DISCUSSION QUESTIONS

1. What was your biggest takeaway from this week's study? What questions do you have after going through the study?
2. Do you or your children have any unique birthmarks? What are some traits that you inherited from your parents?
3. What are some of the caricatures or misconceptions people in your community have about Christians?
4. What is the difference between trying to earn your salvation through good works and doing good because you love Jesus? Why should Christians continue to strive for righteousness even after they are saved and forgiven?
5. What does it mean to "walk in the light"? What is challenging about living in the light?
6. How do you know you are abiding in Jesus? What spiritual practices are helping you abide in Him in your current season of life?
7. What is God asking you to do to show love to the people in your family, your social circle, your workplace, or your community?

PRAYER & ACTION POINT

As a group, spend time thanking God for sending Jesus to enable us to walk in the light of His love. Ask God to give you opportunities this week to show the love of God to people around you.

WEEK 4

MATURITY

LISTEN TO THE SERMON

lwf.org/audio-2105

DISCUSSION QUESTIONS

1. What was your biggest takeaway from this week's study? What questions do you have after going through the study?
2. When you were a child, what were you looking forward to about becoming an adult? Which part of childhood was the most difficult for you to leave behind as you moved into adulthood?
3. How would you describe where you are on your spiritual journey: infancy, childhood, young adulthood, parenthood, or grandparenthood?
4. What is one of the wonders of childhood that you still enjoy? Why is a childlike faith important even for mature believers?
5. In what ways are you a worker and a warrior for the kingdom of God? How has God called you to serve others in your current season of life?
6. When you look back at your spiritual journey, where do you see growth? How are you growing now?
7. What are some spiritual practices in your current season of life that are helping you grow and mature in your faith? What do you feel like God is teaching you right now?

PRAYER & ACTION POINT

With a partner, share where you currently are on your spiritual journey and your next step of faith. Spend time praying for each other.

WEEK 5

THE WORLD

LISTEN TO THE SERMON
lwf.org/audio-2107

DISCUSSION QUESTIONS

1. What was your biggest takeaway from this week's study? What questions do you have after going through the study?
2. Have you ever had an enemy that acted like a friend? What is difficult about ending a friendship?
3. Do you think of the world as an enemy or as a friend? What is the difference?
4. How do you see worldly character, philosophy, purpose, or people making a negative impact on your community? How is what the world believes different from what we believe as Christians?
5. Is it a sin to be tempted? Why is it important for us to know that Jesus was also tempted? What do we learn from Him about temptation?
6. Which type of sin do people in your community struggle with the most: the lust of the flesh, the lust of the eyes, or the pride of life?
7. Why have you chosen to follow Jesus instead of the world? What is something that has happened in your life that only God could do?

PRAYER & ACTION POINT

With a partner, share which of these three (having, being, or doing) you are struggling with the most right now. Pray for one another and remind each other of God's truth.

WEEK 6

THE END

LISTEN TO THE SERMON

lwf.org /audio-2112

DISCUSSION QUESTIONS

1. What was your biggest takeaway from this week's study?
2. What questions do you have after going through the study?
3. What are some things currently happening in the world that are troublesome? Is the world getting better or worse?
4. Of the four factors listed in the Introduction to this chapter, which one is currently the most compelling for you?
5. How do we know we are living in the last days? What are the signs you are looking for?
6. Why is waiting difficult? Do you wish the Second Coming would be immediate or delayed?
7. Where do you see Jesus at work in your community?
8. When you think about meeting Jesus, are you confident or ashamed? What work is He calling you to join in while you are waiting for Him?

PRAYER & ACTION POINT

With a partner, pray for the people in your circle of influence who don't know Jesus. Ask God to give you opportunities to share the Gospel with them.

WEEK 7

HEAVEN

LISTEN TO THE SERMON

lwf.org/audio-2113

DISCUSSION QUESTIONS

1. What was your biggest takeaway from this week's study? What questions do you have after going through the study?
2. When you were younger, what did you think Heaven would be like? What are you looking forward to about Heaven?
3. In what ways are you like your parents? How are your children like you? In what ways do the Christians you know reflect their heavenly Father?
4. When you accepted Christ, how did your identity before God change? What is the difference between being servants or slaves and being children or siblings siblings? (See John 15:15 and Hebrews 2:11-13.)
5. How does our relationship with God change when we think of Him as a Judge or as a Father? Based on your own story, which role describes how you typically relate to God?
6. Based on Day 4, what part of the Christian's destiny do you look forward to the most? What do you wish you knew about the future?
7. What are some things you are doing to prepare to meet Jesus? Who do you want to take to Heaven with you?

PRAYER & ACTION POINT

With a partner, spend time praying for those in your circle of influence who don't know Jesus. Ask God to give you the opportunities, the words, and the courage to share the Gospel with them.

WEEK 8

SALVATION

LISTEN TO THE SERMON
lwf.org/audio-2115

DISCUSSION QUESTIONS

1. What was your biggest takeaway from this week's study? What questions do you have after going through the study?
2. What did you know about church when you were growing up?
3. What does it mean to commit lawlessness? Is it difficult for you to acknowledge that you are a sinner?
4. How does receiving the righteousness of Christ change your identity? How did your life change after you were saved?
5. If you know you are already forgiven, why should you live a good life? Why shouldn't we sin even more?
6. What is the difference between teaching people not to sin and teaching people about Jesus? How have you seen Jesus break the power of sin in your life?
7. If you feel comfortable, briefly share with the group the story of when you were saved. Who were the important people who taught you the Gospel?

PRAYER & ACTION POINT

With a partner, share one of the truths about what it means to be saved that you struggle with or that is difficult for you to really believe. Then pray for each other and for people you know who are not saved.

WEEK 9

LOVE

LISTEN TO THE SERMON

lwf.org/audio-2117

DISCUSSION QUESTIONS

1. What was your biggest takeaway from this week's study? What questions do you have after going through the study?
2. What are some things you love? What are some things you hate?
3. Why is indifference just as damaging as murder or hate? How does indifference impact your community?
4. Which one of these aspects of love from Day 2 is the most meaningful or thought-provoking for you?
5. How valuable is a clear conscience to you? Where does your confidence come from?
6. How do you know when the Holy Spirit is convicting you of sin? How do you discern the voice of God in your life?
7. How have you grieved the Holy Spirit? What bitterness do you need to let go of so that it doesn't continue to grow?

PRAYER & ACTION POINT

With a partner, share what you have learned about love this week and how God is calling you to love those around you. Spend time praying for each other.

WEEK 10

ANTICHRISTS

LISTEN TO THE SERMON

lwf.org/audio-2118`

DISCUSSION QUESTIONS

1. What was your biggest takeaway from this week's study? What questions do you have after going through the study?
2. What is something you used to believe in that you don't believe in anymore? Is it wise to believe something just because someone else tells you it's true?
3. Are all religions the same? How should we interact with people who believe something different from us?
4. What do you look for when you are considering someone's methods, motives, morals, ministry, and message? What do you use to help you discern what is true?
5. Why is it important to study the Bible? How does the Word of God help you resist temptation?
6. What do other religions believe about Jesus? Why is the incarnation of Jesus so important for the Christian faith?
7. How do you recognize the voice of the Holy Spirit in your life? What do you feel like God is prompting you to do?

PRAYER & ACTION POINT

As a group, ask God to help you see the antichrists or false teachings that are impacting your community. Pray for God's protection and for the people who are believing lies. Ask God to give you an opportunity to share the truth of the Gospel with them.

WEEK 11

ASSURANCE

LISTEN TO THE SERMON
lwf.org/audio-2119

DISCUSSION QUESTIONS

1. What was your biggest takeaway from this week's study? What questions do you have after going through the study?
2. What does it take for you to be sure something is real? What kind of proof do you look for?
3. Why is it important to believe that the blood of Jesus atones for your sin and that the water cleanses you from sin? What is the difference between salvation and sanctification?
4. Why do we need the Holy Spirit in our lives? How do you know the Holy Spirit is at work?
5. How has the Holy Spirit confirmed in you that you belong to God? What spiritual practices have helped you discern the voice of the Spirit in your life?
6. When have you felt the Holy Spirit speaking through you to others?
7. How has the Holy Spirit worked through you to help others?

PRAYER & ACTION POINT

As a group, thank God for sending Jesus to atone for our sins and cleanse us from all unrighteousness. Pray for those in your circle of influence who don't know Jesus and ask God to give you opportunities to share the Gospel with them.

DISCUSSION NOTES

DISCUSSION NOTES

DISCUSSION NOTES

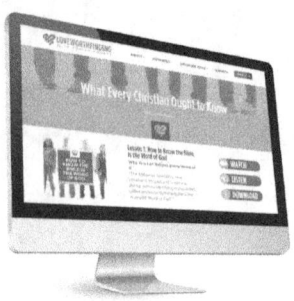

VISIT US ONLINE AT LWF.ORG

Love Worth Finding Ministries with Adrian Rogers is pleased to be able to bring you this Bible study. If you have found it helpful, we suggest you go to our website, **lwf.org**.

Peruse our "find answers" **Q&A** "about my life, about our world and "about God." Sign up for an **email challenge** that brings encouragement to your inbox. Engage in a study from our **Biblical Learning Center**. Or go to the **LWF Store** for print and digital resources for yourself and those you love.

Through broadcast, print and digital media, our reach is global. Our mission is to help people find the greatest Love worth finding, Jesus Christ, and to help those who already know Jesus grow in the faith.

Put Love Worth Finding in the palm of your hand with the **MyLWF App**.

Here you'll find audio and video messages from Pastor Adrian Rogers, our daily devotional, and special programs such as our "Conversations that Matter" interview-format program on biblical topics and our "Voices" audio theater programs.

The **MyLWF App** includes programming in several languages. And you can learn how to partner in Love Worth Finding's global mission to bring people to Christ and help them grow in the faith.

Scan the QR code below or search for the heart-shaped **MyLWF App** in your favorite app store to download it today.

ADDITIONAL BIBLE STUDIES IN THIS SERIES

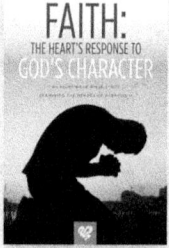

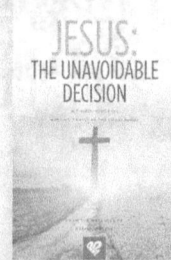

For these and other resources, visit **lwf.org**/store or call **(800) 274-5683**

www.ingramcontent.com/pod-product-compliance
Lightning Source LLC
Chambersburg PA
CBHW070528010526
44110CB00050B/2323